The Great Big BINGO Book

BINGO Games for ESL Learners

Nina Ito and Anne Berry

PRO LINGUA ⬤ ASSOCIATES

Pro Lingua Associates, Publishers
P.O. Box 1348
Brattleboro, Vermont 05302-1348 USA
Office: 802 257 7779
Orders: 800 366 4775
E-mail: prolingu@sover.net
SAN: 216-0579
Webstore: www.ProLinguaAssociates.com

At *Pro Lingua*
our objective is to foster an approach
to learning and teaching that we call
interplay, *the **inter**action of language*
learners and teachers with their materials,
with the language and culture,
and with each other in active, creative
*and productive **play**.*

Copyright © 2001 by Nina Ito and Anne Berry

ISBN 0-86647-140-5

All rights reserved. No part of this publication may be reproduced or transmitted in any form or by any means, electronic, mechanical, photocopying, recording or other, or stored in an information storage or retrieval system without permission in writing from the publisher. However, permission to copy is granted by the publisher as follows:

All pages with teacher's cards in the Teacher's Notes or BINGO boards and "chips" may be copied for classroom use.

This book was designed by the authors with the assistance of Judy Ashkenaz and Arthur A. Burrows. It was printed and bound by Capital City Press in Montpelier, Vermont. The illustrations are by Anne Berry or are clipart selected from a variety of sources.

Printed in the United States of America
Third printing 2005.
7000 copies in print.

Table of Contents

Proficiency Levels: ❶ Beginning; ❷ Lower Intermediate; ❸ Upper Intermediate; ❹ Advanced

Section 4 – Writing

Section 5 – Cultural Topics *(Holidays)*   105

Appendix

Acknowledgments

We would like to thank our colleagues at the American Language Institute (California State University, Long Beach), the Center for Language Education and Development (Georgetown University, Washington, D.C.), the Atlantic Group (Madrid, Spain), and our former classmates in the Division of English as an International Language (University of Illinois, Urbana-Champaign) for the extremely useful feedback they gave us. We would also like to thank our families and friends for giving us the time and encouragement we needed to finish this project.

Nina Ito
Anne Berry

Editor's Pronouncement on Pronouns

In this book, we at Pro Lingua Associates are offering a solution to the vexing "he/she" pronoun problem. We have come to the conclusion that when a pronominal reference is made to a third person, and that person is indefinite (and hence, gender is unknown or unimportant), we will use the third person plural forms, *they, them,* and *their(s).* We are fully aware that historically these forms represent grammatical plurality. However, there are clear instances in the English language where the third person plural form is used to refer to a preceding indefinite, grammatically singular pronoun.

Examples:

> Everyone says this, don't **they**?
> Nobody agrees with us, but we will ignore **them**.

If you will accept the examples above, it is not a major step to find the following acceptable:

> The learner of English should find this easier because **they** can avoid the confusion of *"he"* or *"she,"* the awkwardness of *"he or she"* or *"s/he,"* and the implicit sexism of using *"he"* for everybody.

So in this book, you will find instructions such as, *When a student has marked three squares in a row, they should call out "BINGO!"* The reader of this text may disagree with our solution, but we ask them to blame us, the publishers, not the authors.

Languages do change, and the usage of gender-marked pronouns is changing. This is our solution, and we encourage you to try it out. And we invite your comments.

RCC for PLA

To The Teacher

Teachers of ESL/EFL spend countless hours thinking up new ways to teach the traditional components of the English language. They ask, "How can I present this point so that the students will understand? How can we practice this vocabulary in a way that's enjoyable for these students? How can I motivate this group so that they want to work?" The games in this book provide practice with structures and topics that can be found on any syllabus, using a game that is known around the world, but they do it in ways that are varied, creative and fun.

Traditional BINGO

Traditional BINGO involves a caller, who calls out numbers and letters in different combinations (B9, G77, etc.), and players, who have BINGO cards (a 5x5-square grid labeled B-I-N-G-O across the top and filled in with a random selection of numbers.) Players listen to the combinations called and mark the numbers that appear on their boards. The first player to mark five squares in a row (horizontally, vertically, or diagonally), calls out "BINGO!" and wins.

B	I	N	G	O
2	21	44	61	88
17	33	48	79	81
14	36	50	77	91
9	28	52	63	95
3	39	57	68	82

← Bingo!

Some of the games in this book are quite similar to traditional BINGO – the main difference being, instead of number/letter combinations, the teacher calls out vocabulary items which the students find and mark on their boards. However, most of the games are very different – the students must do much more than listen to a word, find it on the board, and mark the square. Each game comes with its own set of instructions, but some of the game types are described on the next page.

The Games in This Book

The games are categorized into skill/topic areas. The five sections are vocabulary, pronunciation, grammar, writing, and cultural topics. Within each section the games are labeled according to their levels of difficulty. These numbers are indicated in the procedure descriptions at the beginning of each game.

❶ Beginning
❷ Lower Intermediate
❸ Upper Intermediate
❹ Advanced

All of the games can be used in the context of an intensive English program, and most can be used in other ESL contexts within the United States and in EFL contexts around the world.

"Traditional" BINGO Games – Some of the games involve more difficult variations on the standard instructions for BINGO. For example, in "Weather BINGO" and "Clothing BINGO", instead of saying a word, the teacher can give a definition or description, and the students mark their boards. In "'So…'/'Neither…' BINGO", the teacher makes a statement, and the students must find the appropriate response and mark their boards. In "Go, Went, Gone BINGO", the teacher says a verb; the students conjugate the verb and then strategize about where to write it on the board.

"Task" BINGO Games – In these games the students are required to do something before they can mark a square. For example, in "Valentine's Day BINGO", the students write a poem to mark the square. In "Scavenger Hunt BINGO", they explore different areas of the school and mark squares that they've completed. In "Punctuation BINGO", the students must punctuate sentences before they can mark their squares.

"Talking" BINGO Games – In this type of game, the students have to talk to people before they can mark a square. For example, in "Ice Breaker BINGO," the students interview their class-mates until they find people with certain characteristics. In "Thanksgiving BINGO," the students survey native speakers about their favorite Thanksgiving foods until they hear the foods on their boards.

"Testing" BINGO Games – In these games, all of the students have the same board. If they all get BINGO at the same time, the teacher knows they have acquired the necessary skills/knowledge. For example, in "Pronunciation BINGO", if the students hear the minimal pairs correctly, they will all get BINGO at the same time. In "Classroom BINGO", if the students have investigated the idioms well, they will all get BINGO at the same time.

Preparation

Because the games are so varied, teachers should read the Teacher's Notes and the Student's Page(s) carefully ahead of time, think through the process and decide whether a game will be appropriate for a particular class at a particular time. Then they will need to prepare the necessary materials. (Teachers should not cut up the book itself, but rather always photocopy the pages first and then cut up the boards, cards and chips.)

The Boards: Instructions for each game specify whether every student gets a copy of the same board or whether there are different boards to be photocopied. In some cases, the teacher must prepare the board before making copies by adding information to some squares. In other cases, the students will need time to prepare their boards before playing. Some games require that the students have a copy of the board to write on, but with other games, the teacher can choose to mount or laminate the boards to make a permanent set. The games that require multiple boards can be organized in various ways. If there are eight (or fewer) students in the class, each student gets one of the boards provided in the book. If there are more than eight students, some alternatives are:

- The teacher is the caller. Some or all of the students play in pairs, each pair with one of the eight boards provided.

- The teacher makes more than one copy of each board, so that there is one board for each student. The students play individually, but several students may get BINGO at the same time.

- The students play in groups of five. One student is the caller. The rest play, with each one using one of the eight boards provided.

- Before class, the teacher cuts apart one or more of the boards and reassembles the pieces in different arrangements to make as many new boards as necessary so that each student can play, and everybody will have a different board.

The Cards: Instructions for each game describe how to prepare the cards (when cards are necessary). The teacher can choose to mount or laminate the cards to make a permanent set. In some cases, there are more cards than there are squares on a board, but every card corresponds to an answer that is on at least some of the boards.

The Chips: Instructions for each game will specify whether chips are necessary. There is a page of chips at the back of the book that the teacher can photocopy and cut apart (mounted and/or laminated if so desired). Alternatively, students can use candy, seeds, pennies, etc., to mark their boards. Or, in some cases, they can mark squares using a pencil, making a different shaped mark each time the game is played, or erasing the marks each time and starting over.

This book is the product of many years of challenging our students with all sorts of tasks in enjoyable new ways. We hope you enjoy the games as much as we do!

		Jello Salad		
Pumpkin Pie	Potato Salad		Sweet Potatoes	Apple Pie
Cranberry Sauce	Bread	Carrots	Rolls	Yams or Candied Yams
Ham	Stuffed Mushrooms	Turkey	Corn or Creamed Corn	Gravy
Stuffing or Dressing	Corn Bread	Broccoli	Biscuits	Green Beans or Green Bean Casserole
Pecan Pie	Green Salad	Mashed Potatoes	Fruit Salad	Mincemeat Pie

The
Great
Big
BINGO
Book

"Nice to Meet You" BINGO *(Functions)*

This game is used to test students' knowledge of easy functions.

The BINGO Boards

There are eight boards for this game. The students may play individually or in pairs. If there are more than 16 students in the class, extra boards may be photocopied. In this case, several students should get BINGO at the same time.

The Cards

Before class, the teacher should photocopy and cut apart the cards below. The teacher can glue each rectangle to an index card to make a permanent set.

The Procedure

❶ The teacher mixes up the cards and places them face down on the table. The teacher draws the top card from the stack and asks the question or reads the sentence. The students look at their boards, and if they have the correct response, they mark the appropriate square. For example, if the teacher says, "Nice to meet you," the student marks, "Nice to meet you, too." When a student has marked three squares in a row (horizontally, vertically or diagonally), they should call out "BINGO!" To confirm the win, the student tells the class which three they have in a row while the teacher verifies that these are correct.

"Nice to Meet You" **BINGO**	What's your phone number? *(202) 985-1805*	What time is it? *Twelve-thirty*
How are you? *Fine, thanks.*	How do you spell your last name? *It's G-O-M-E-Z.*	Nice to meet you. *Nice to meet you, too.*
See you later. *Bye!*	Thanks. *You're welcome.*	How much is it? *50 cents.*
When's your birthday? *November 11th*	Where are you from? *China*	What's your address? *714 Park Street*
Where's the restroom? *Down the hall.*	Would you like some coffee? *Yes, please.*	What do you do? *I'm a student.*

Vocabulary 1

"Nice to Meet You" BINGO

Listen to the teacher. The teacher will ask a question or say a sentence. If you see the answer on this board, mark the square. When you have three in a row, call out "BINGO!"

Down the hall.	Yes, please.	You're welcome.
November 11th	Twelve-thirty	It's G-O-M-E-Z.
I'm a student.	(202) 985-1805	Nice to meet you, too.

- ✂ -

"Nice to Meet You" BINGO

Listen to the teacher. The teacher will ask a question or say a sentence. If you see the answer on this board, mark the square. When you have three in a row, call out "BINGO!"

Nice to meet you, too.	You're welcome.	Bye!
50 cents	I'm a student.	Down the hall.
Yes, please.	Twelve-thirty	It's G-O-M-E-Z.

"Nice to Meet You" BINGO

Listen to the teacher. The teacher will ask a question or say a sentence. If you see the answer on this board, mark the square. When you have three in a row, call out "BINGO!"

50 cents	714 Park Street	Nice to meet you, too.
November 11th	You're welcome.	Fine, thanks.
China	Bye!	Twelve-thirty

---- ✂ ----

"Nice to Meet You" BINGO

Listen to the teacher. The teacher will ask a question or say a sentence. If you see the answer on this board, mark the square. When you have three in a row, call out "BINGO!"

Yes, please.	It's G-O-M-E-Z.	50 cents
Fine, thanks.	China	You're welcome.
714 Park Street	Nice to meet you, too.	(202) 985-1805

Vocabulary 3

"Nice to Meet You" BINGO

Listen to the teacher. The teacher will ask a question or say a sentence. If you see the answer on this board, mark the square. When you have three in a row, call out "BINGO!"

November 11th	714 Park Street	Yes, please.
It's G-O-M-E-Z.	Twelve-thirty	(202) 985-1805
Fine, thanks.	Nice to meet you, too.	You're welcome.

- ✂ -

"Nice to Meet You" BINGO

Listen to the teacher. The teacher will ask a question or say a sentence. If you see the answer on this board, mark the square. When you have three in a row, call out "BINGO!"

China	714 Park Street	Down the hall.
Yes, please.	I'm a student.	50 cents
Bye!	Fine, thanks.	(202) 985-1805

"Nice to Meet You" BINGO

Listen to the teacher. The teacher will ask a question or say a sentence. If you see the answer on this board, mark the square. When you have three in a row, call out "BINGO!"

It's G-O-M-E-Z.	(202) 985-1805	Twelve-thirty
Fine, thanks.	Nice to meet you, too.	Bye!
You're welcome.	50 cents	November 11th

- ✂ -

"Nice to Meet You" BINGO

Listen to the teacher. The teacher will ask a question or say a sentence. If you see the answer on this board, mark the square. When you have three in a row, call out "BINGO!"

I'm a student.	Yes, please.	Down the hall.
714 Park Street	China	November 11th
50 cents	You're welcome	Bye!

Vocabulary   5

Action BINGO

This game is used to test students' knowledge of action verb vocabulary.

The BINGO Boards
There are eight boards for this game. The students may play individually or in pairs. If there are more than 16 students in the class, extra boards may be photocopied. In this case, several students should get BINGO at the same time.

The Cards
Before class, the teacher should photocopy and cut apart the cards below. The teacher can glue each rectangle to an index card to make a permanent set.

The Procedure
❶ The teacher mixes up the cards and places them face down on the table. The teacher draws the top card from the stack and mimes the action (e.g., "sleeping"). The students look at their boards, and if they have the mimed gerund, they mark the appropriate square. When a student has marked four squares in a row (horizontally, vertically or diagonally), they should call out "BINGO!" To confirm the win, the student tells the class which four they have in a row while the teacher verifies that these are correct.

ACTION BINGO	Instructions: Mime the words. Students mark their boards.	swimming	walking
reading	sleeping	dancing	driving
kissing	talking	drinking	crying
taking a shower	brushing your teeth	watching TV	jumping
sewing	writing	falling	laughing
sitting	sweeping	running	eating

Action BINGO

Watch the teacher. The teacher will do an action. If you see the action on this board, mark the square. When you have four in a row, call out "BINGO!"

sleeping	swimming	reading	running
sitting	falling	sewing	watching TV
brushing your teeth	crying	talking	driving
sweeping	laughing	writing	jumping

- ✂ -

Action BINGO

Watch the teacher. The teacher will do an action. If you see the action on this board, mark the square. When you have four in a row, call out "BINGO!"

swimming	talking	sleeping	crying
eating	walking	dancing	kissing
watching TV	drinking	taking a shower	laughing
running	sewing	falling	sitting

Vocabulary   7

Action BINGO

Watch the teacher. The teacher will do an action. If you see the action on this board, mark the square. When you have four in a row, call out "BINGO!"

dancing	walking	swimming	eating
watching TV	taking a shower	drinking	kissing
falling	writing	sewing	jumping
running	sweeping	sitting	laughing

- ✂ -

Action BINGO

Watch the teacher. The teacher will do an action. If you see the action on this board, mark the square. When you have four in a row, call out "BINGO!"

laughing	sitting	sweeping	running
reading	eating	swimming	walking
watching TV	sewing	writing	falling
sleeping	dancing	driving	talking

Reproducible for classroom use. Copyright © 2001 Nina Ito and Anne Berry.

Action BINGO

Watch the teacher. The teacher will do an action. If you see the action on this board, mark the square. When you have four in a row, call out "BINGO!"

sweeping	laughing	writing	jumping
brushing your teeth	crying	drinking	watching TV
kissing	driving	dancing	sleeping
walking	swimming	eating	reading

- ✂ -

Action BINGO

Watch the teacher. The teacher will do an action. If you see the action on this board, mark the square. When you have four in a row, call out "BINGO!"

brushing your teeth	running	sweeping	sitting
jumping	eating	laughing	falling
kissing	drinking	crying	taking a shower
sleeping	walking	reading	dancing

Reproducible for classroom use. Copyright © 2001 Nina Ito and Anne Berry.   **Vocabulary   9**

Action BINGO

Watch the teacher. The teacher will do an action. If you see the action on this board, mark the square. When you have four in a row, call out "BINGO!"

reading	eating	swimming	walking
sleeping	dancing	driving	kissing
talking	drinking	crying	taking a shower
brushing your teeth	watching TV	jumping	sewing

- ✂ -

Action BINGO

Watch the teacher. The teacher will do an action. If you see the action on this board, mark the square. When you have four in a row, call out "BINGO!"

running	falling	watching TV	drinking
sweeping	writing	brushing your teeth	talking
sitting	sewing	taking a shower	kissing
laughing	jumping	crying	driving

Reproducible for classroom use. Copyright © 2001 Nina Ito and Anne Berry.

lettuce	This is a green, leafy vegetable that grows into a head-shaped ball. It is most often eaten in salads.	shrimp	This is a type of shellfish. When it is cooked it is small and pink. We eat them alone, hot or cold, or add them to dishes or sauces.
cucumbers	This is a vegetable with green skin and a crisp, white inside. It is long and fat with seeds down the middle, and usually eaten raw.	rice	This is a grain. It is small and either white or brown. It is usually boiled and served with meats and vegetables.
cabbage	This is a green, leafy vegetable that grows into a head-shaped ball. It is most often boiled or cured and served on the side.		
cauliflower	This is a vegetable that grows on the ground. It is white and looks like a little tree with a stem and a rounded, crumbly top.		
tomatoes	This is a juicy red fruit that grows on a vine. It is often prepared as a vegetable, added to salads or cooked into dishes and sauces.		
peppers	This is a crisp, hollow vegetable that comes in many colors. They can be eaten raw or cooked. The hot ones can add spice to a dish.		
onions	This is a vegetable that grows underground. It has white layers, yellow or pink skin, and a strong flavor. It can make a chef cry.		
olives	This is the fruit of a tree. They are small, with pits, and can be picked green or black. They can be cured or pressed for their oil.		

Food BINGO

Fill in each blank square with a type of food from the list below. Then listen to the teacher. Mark the square with the type of food you hear. When you have four in a row, call out "BINGO!"

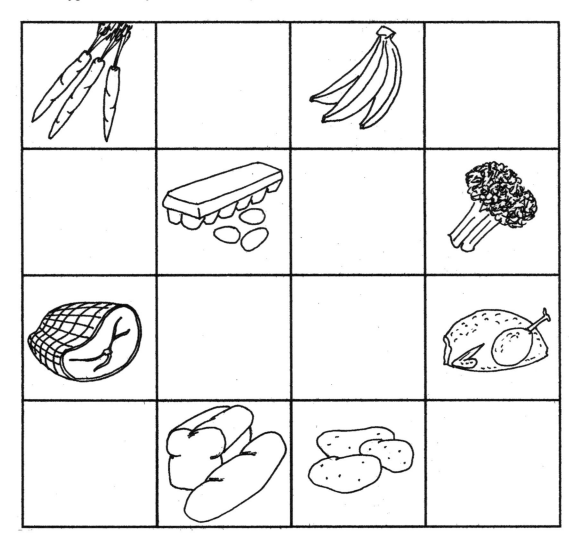

Foods

Rice	Tomatoes	Strawberries
Pasta	Peppers	Milk
Green beans	Onions	Yogurt
Peas	Olives	Cheese
Asparagus	Apples	Chicken
Lettuce	Oranges	Beef
Cucumbers	Lemons	Lamb
Cabbage	Pears	Fish
Cauliflower	Melon	Shrimp

Body Parts BINGO

These games test students' knowledge of words for body parts.

The BINGO Board

There is one board for this game. Eight of the squares are already filled in with body parts. The students fill in the other eight squares with their choices from the list below the board or from another list that the teacher provides. In this way, every student has a different board.

The Cards

Before class, the teacher should photocopy and cut apart the cards on the next pages. There are extra cards in case the teacher wants to add more body vocabulary to the game. The teacher can glue each rectangle to an index card to make a permanent set.

The Procedure

❶ Game 1: The teacher makes a copy of the board for each student. The students read the instructions and begin by filling in the blank squares on the grid. The teacher mixes up the cards and places them face down on the table. The teacher draws the top card from the stack and reads the <u>name</u> of the body part. The students look at their boards, and if they have that body part, they mark the appropriate square. When a student has marked four squares in a row (horizontally, vertically or diagonally), they should call out "BINGO!" To confirm the win, the student tells the class which four they have in a row while the teacher verifies that these are correct.

❷ Game 2: See Game 1, except that the teacher reads the <u>description</u> of the body part. The students look at their boards, and if they have that body part, they mark the appropriate square. When a student has marked four squares in a row (horizontally, vertically or diagonally), they should call out "BINGO!" To confirm the win, the student tells the class which four they have in a row while the teacher verifies that these are correct.

Cards for Body Parts BINGO		neck	This part of the body connects the head to the shoulders.
knees	These are joints -- the places where the legs bend.	chest	This is the front part of the torso.
thigh	This is the upper part of the leg.	back	This is the back part of the torso.
eyes	These are found on the face. We use them to see.	arms	These extremities start at the shoulders. We use them to hug.
ears	These are found on the side of the head. We use them to hear.	wrists	These are joints - the places where the hands meet the arms.
elbow	This is a joint - the place where the arm bends.	hands	These are found at the end of the arms. We use them to clap.

shoulders	These are joints – the places where the arms meet the body.	fingers	There are ten of these. They are found on the hands.
thumb	This is the largest finger, separate from the other four.	palm	This is the flat part in the center of the hand.
waist	This is the middle of the body, between the chest and the hips. It's where we wear a belt.	stomach	This is an organ inside the body where food is digested.
face	This is the area of the head that has the eyes, nose, and mouth.	hips	These are joints - the places where the legs meet the body.
hair	This is a soft material that grows from the head.	buttocks	These are the fleshy areas below the back. We sit on them.
forehead	This is the part of the face found under the hairline and above the eyebrows.	legs	These extremities start at the hips. We use them to walk.
eyebrows	These are the lines of hair that grow above the eyes.	ankles	These are joints - the places where the legs meet the feet.
eyelashes	These are the hairs that grow on the eyelids.	feet	These are found at the end of the legs. We stand on them all day.
eyelids	This is the skin that covers your eyes when you sleep.	toes	There are ten of these. They are found on the feet.
nose	This is found on the front of the face. We use it to smell.		
cheeks	These soft round areas are found on either side of the nose and mouth.		
mouth	This is found below the nose. We use it to eat.		
teeth	These are hard and white, and they are found inside the mouth.		
jaw	This is the bone at the bottom of the skull. It moves when we chew.		
chin	This is the center point at the bottom of the face, below the mouth.		

Body Parts BINGO

Fill in each blank square with a body part from the list below. Then listen to the teacher. Mark the square with the body part you hear. When you have four in a row, call out "BINGO!"

Body Parts

Face	Teeth	Fingers
Hair	Jaw	Palms
Forehead	Chin	Stomach
Eyebrows	Neck	Hips
Eyelashes	Chest	Buttocks
Eyelids	Back	Legs
Nose	Arms	Ankles
Cheeks	Wrists	Feet
Mouth	Hands	Toes

Vocabulary 17

Weather BINGO

These games practice recognition and use of vocabulary associated with the weather.

The BINGO Board

There is one board for this game. Eight of the squares are already filled in with types of weather. The students fill in the other eight squares with their choices from the list below the board. In this way, every student has a different board.

The Cards

Before class, the teacher should photocopy and cut apart the cards on the next page. The teacher can glue each rectangle to an index card to make a permanent set.

The Procedure

❶ Game 1: The teacher makes a copy of the board for each student. The students read the instructions and begin by filling in the blank squares on the grid. The teacher mixes up the cards and places them face down on the table. The caller (at first the teacher, later a student) draws the top card from the stack and reads the word. The students look at their boards, and if they have the picture, they mark the appropriate square. When a student has marked four squares in a row (horizontally, vertically or diagonally), they should call out "BINGO!" To confirm the win, the student tells the class which four they have in a row while the teacher verifies that these are correct.

❷ Game 2: See Game 1, except that the students fill in the empty squares as homework, and come to class with just the grid. The vocabulary list at the bottom of the page is either folded back or cut off. The caller randomly chooses a card and reads the word. The students mark the appropriate squares until someone calls out "BINGO!"

❷ Game 3: See Game 2, except that the caller reads the sentence on the card about the type of weather. For example, the teacher says, "What a day! Will it ever stop raining?" and the students mark "rainy."

❷ Game 4: The students play in pairs. The partners alternate picking squares and making a sentence with that type of weather. The teacher circulates, acting as judge. If a sentence is correct, the student can mark that square on their own grid. When a student has marked four squares in a row (horizontally, vertically or diagonally), they should call out "BINGO!"

Reproducible for classroom use. Copyright © 2001 Nina Ito and Anne Berry.

	hot	"This seems like the hottest summer ever."		sunny	"Let's go to the beach. There's not a cloud in the sky."
	warm	"Ah! The first days of spring have such a nice temperature."		partly cloudy	"When the sun is out, it's nice, but when it goes behind a cloud, it's cool."
	cool	"Put on your jacket. It's a cool fall day."		cloudy	"The sky is so gray. I can't see any blue sky."
	cold	"If you think it's cold in December, just wait until January."		rainy	"What a day! Will it ever stop raining?"
	freezing	"Brrr. It's two degrees below zero."		icy	"Be careful today. All the water has frozen and turned to ice."
	tornado	"April is tornado season in Kansas."		snowing	"The perfect winter day is when everything is covered with white."
	lightning	"Quick! Let's get off the golf course. I just saw lightning on the horizon."		windy	"Hold on to your hat so the wind doesn't blow it away."
	dry	"My skin is so dry in this weather."		foggy	"There is so much water in the air. I can't see ten feet in front of me."

Vocabulary 19

Weather BINGO

Fill in each blank square with a type of weather. Then listen to the teacher. Mark the square with the weather you hear. When you have four in a row, call out "BINGO!"

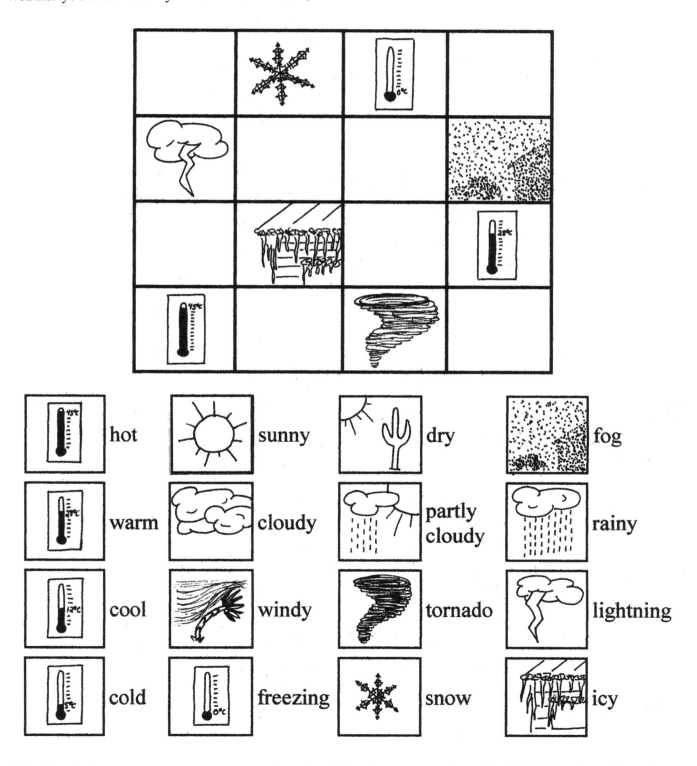

Reproducible for classroom use. Copyright © 2001 Nina Ito and Anne Berry.

Clothing BINGO

These games practice recognition and use of vocabulary associated with clothing and descriptions of clothing.

The BINGO Board
There are eight boards for this game. The students may play individually or in pairs. If there are more than 16 students in the class, extra boards may be photocopied. In this case, several students should get BINGO at the same time.

The Cards
Before class, the teacher should photocopy and cut apart the cards below and on the next page. The teacher can glue each rectangle to an index card to make a permanent set.

The Procedure
❶ Game 1: The teacher mixes up the cards and places them face down on the table. The teacher draws the top card from the stack and reads the <u>name</u> of the article of clothing. The students look at their boards, and if they have that article of clothing, they mark the appropriate square. When a student has marked five squares in a row (horizontally, vertically or diagonally), they should call out "BINGO!" To confirm the win, the student tells the class which five they have in a row while the teacher verifies that these are correct.

❷ Game 2: See Game 1, except that the teacher reads the <u>description</u> of the article of clothing pictured: e.g., "This article of clothing has sleeves." The students look at their boards, and if they have an article of clothing with sleeves, they mark the appropriate square. When a student has marked five squares in a row (horizontally, vertically or diagonally), they should call out "BINGO!" To confirm the win, the student explains why they marked those five squares: e.g., "I marked the shirt because it has sleeves." In this variation, more than one answer may be correct; a shirt, a jacket, a suit, etc., all have sleeves.

	Clothing Bingo			hat	This article of clothing is worn on the head.
	scarf	This article of clothing is often worn around the neck.		cap	This article of clothing keeps the head warm.
	gloves	This article of clothing is worn to keep the hands warm.		tie	This article of clothing is usually worn by men.
	boots	This article of clothing is worn on the feet.		shoes	This article of clothing is made of leather.
	sandals	This article of clothing is worn in the summer.		gym shoes	This article of clothing has laces.

Vocabulary 21

	stockings	This article of clothing is worn by women.		socks	This article of clothing is made of wool or cotton.
	long dress or gown	This article of clothing reaches the floor.		jacket	This article of clothing has a hood.
	pajamas	This article of clothing is worn at night.		slippers	This article of clothing is worn inside the house.
	jeans	This article of clothing is made of denim.		shorts	This article of clothing covers only part of the legs.
	turtleneck shirt	This article of clothing has a high collar.		shirt	This article of clothing has long sleeves and a collar.
	t-shirt	This article of clothing has short sleeves and no buttons.		pants	This article of clothing has pockets.
	vest	This article of clothing has buttons.		tank top	This article of clothing is sleeveless.
	suit	This article of clothing has 2 or 3 pieces.		sweats or sweat suit	This article of clothing is worn when exercising.
	bathrobe	This article of clothing can be used like a towel.		bathing suit	This article of clothing gets wet.
	coat	This article of clothing is worn in the winter.		sweater	This article of clothing is thick and warm.
	underwear	This article of clothing is worn under the other clothes.		belt	This article of clothing has a buckle.

Reproducible for classroom use. Copyright © 2001 Nina Ito and Anne Berry.

Sports BINGO

These games test students' knowledge of vocabulary associated with sports.

The BINGO Board

There are eight boards for this game. The students may play individually or in pairs. If there are more than 16 students in the class, extra boards may be photocopied. In this case, several students should get BINGO at the same time.

The Cards

Before class, the teacher should photocopy and cut apart the cards below and on the next page. The teacher can glue each rectangle to an index card to make a permanent set.

The Procedure

❶ Game 1: The teacher mixes up the cards and places them face down on the table. The teacher draws the top card from the stack and reads the <u>name</u> of the sport. The students look at their boards, and if they have that sport, they mark the appropriate square. When a student has marked four squares in a row (horizontally, vertically or diagonally), they should call out "BINGO!" To confirm the win, the student tells the class which four they have in a row while the teacher verifies that these are correct.

❷ Game 2: See Game 1, except that the teacher reads the <u>list</u> of terms and equipment used with a certain sport: e.g., "Steal, slide, bat, home run." The students look at their boards, and if they have the sport that uses those terms and equipment, they mark the appropriate square. When a student has marked four squares in a row (horizontally, vertically or diagonally), they should call out "BINGO!" To confirm the win, the student tells the class which four they have in a row while the teacher verifies that these are correct.

Cards for Sports BINGO

	Golf	birdie, putter, chip, gallery
	Tennis	ace, love, doubles, backhand
	Soccer	midfielder, yellow card, penalty kick

	Basketball	rebound, traveling, key, lay-up
	Football	punt, quarterback, shoulder pads, field goal
	Baseball	steal, slide, home run, bat
	Swimming	butterfly, lanes, kick, freestyle

	Diving	board, pool, tuck		Gymnastics	beam, horse, rings, floor routine
	Volleyball	net, side-out, spike, dig, serve		Surfing	wetsuit, pipeline, board, hang ten
	Skiing	downhill, poles, lift, slalom		Ice Skating	axel, pairs, spin, rink
	Bowling	strike, lane, pins, spare		Martial Arts	judo, karate, jujitsu, tae kwan do
	Ice Hockey	puck, stick, icing, goalie		Sailing	downwind, mast, starboard, capsize
	Wrestling	pin, take down, mat		Boxing	ring, jab, round, knockout
	Badminton	shuttlecock, rackets, net, volley		Cycling	gears, helmet, pedals
	Track and Field	sprint, relay, mile, hurdle		Instructions: Read the sport, or the list of terms and equipment. The students mark their boards.	

Reproducible for classroom use. Copyright © 2001 Nina Ito and Anne Berry.

Sports BINGO

Listen to the teacher. If you see the correct sport on this board, mark the square. When you have four in a row, call out "BINGO!"

- ✂ -

Sports BINGO

Listen to the teacher. If you see the correct sport on this board, mark the square. When you have four in a row, call out "BINGO!"

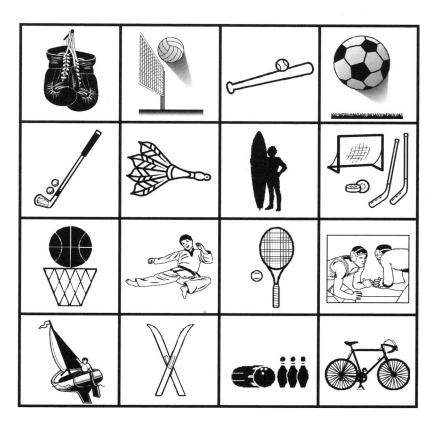

Vocabulary 29

Sports
BINGO

Listen o the teacher. If you see the correct sport on this board, mark the square. When you have four in a row, call out "BINGO!"

Sports
BINGO

Listen to the teacher. If you see the correct sport on this board, mark the square. When you have four in a row, call out "BINGO!"

Reproducible for classroom use. Copyright © 2001 Nina Ito and Anne Berry.

Sports BINGO

Listen to the teacher. If you see the correct sport on this board, mark the square. When you have four in a row, call out "BINGO!"

Sports BINGO

Listen to the teacher. If you see the correct sport on this board, mark the square. When you have four in a row, call out "BINGO!"

Vocabulary   31

Sports *BINGO*

Listen to the teacher. If you see the correct sport on this board, mark the square. When you have four in a row, call out "BINGO!"

Sports *BINGO*

Listen to the teacher. If you see the correct sport on this board, mark the square. When you have four in a row, call out "BINGO!"

Gestures BINGO

These games test students' knowledge of gestures used in the United States.

The BINGO Board

There are eight boards for this game. The students may play individually or in pairs. If there are more than 16 students in the class, extra boards may be photocopied. In this case, several students should get BINGO at the same time.

The Cards

Before class, the teacher should photocopy and cut apart the cards below and on the next page. The teacher can glue each rectangle to an index card to make a permanent set.

The Procedure

❷ ❸ Game 1: The teacher mixes up the cards and places them face down on the table. The teacher draws the top card from the stack and does the gesture (e.g., makes a circle with thumb and index finger, and holds up hand to mean "O.K."). The students look at their boards, and if they have the gesture, they mark the appropriate square. When a student has marked four squares in a row (horizontally, vertically or diagonally), they should call out "BINGO!" To confirm the win, the student tells the class which four they have in a row while the teacher verifies that these are correct.

Vocabulary   33

GESTURES BINGO	Come here. *(Beckon with finger.)*	Go away. *(Move back of hand outward.)*
Stop! *(Hold up hand with palm facing outward.)*	You're crazy. *(Make a circling motion with finger near temple.)*	(money) *(Rub thumb and fingers together.)*
I don't know. *(Shrug shoulders.)*	I can't hear. *(Cup hand around ear.)*	Be quiet! *(Raise one index finger in front of lips.)*
Look at that! (pointing) *(Point at something with index finger.)*	Shame on you. *(Shake index finger toward the class.)*	Good luck/Let's hope. *(Cross index finger and middle finger.)*
Phew! (relief) *(Wipe brow with back of hand.)*	Darn! (disappointment) *(Snap fingers and move arm downward diagonally.)*	YES! (excitement) *(Make a fist and pump arm downward once.)*
O.K. *(Make a circle with thumb and index finger. Hold up hand.)*	No, thanks. *(Shake hand side to side in front of you – palm outward.)*	Me? *(Point to chest.)*
It's over my head. *(Pass a flat hand over your head from front to back.)*	Ho-hum (impatience) *(Drum fingers of one hand on table.)*	Just a minute. *(Raise index finger.)*
Yes. (affirmative) *(Nod head up and down.)*	No. (negative) *(Shake head side to side.)*	Yes, Sir! *(Salute from temple.)*
It's cold. *(Cross arms and rub opposite arm.)*	It's hot. *(Fan yourself with one hand.)*	Yesterday (past time) *(Point backwards over shoulder.)*
Bad idea. *(Show thumbs-down sign.)*	Good idea. *(Show thumbs-up sign.)*	Calm down! *(Use a slow repeated downward motion with two palms.)*

Gestures BINGO

Watch the teacher. The teacher will do a gesture. If you see the gesture on this board, mark the square. When you have four in a row, call out "BINGO!"

Come here.	No, thanks.	Go away.	You're crazy.
(money)	I don't know.	Shame on you.	Good luck or Let's hope.
Phew! (relief)	Stop!	YES! (excitement)	O.K.
Be quiet!	Look at that! (pointing)	I can't hear.	Darn! (disappointment)

- ✂ -

Gestures BINGO

Watch the teacher. The teacher will do a gesture. If you see the gesture on this board, mark the square. When you have four in a row, call out "BINGO!"

Calm down!	Just a minute.	No. (negative)	Me?
YES! (excitement)	It's cold.	Good idea.	Yes, Sir!
O.K.	Yesterday. (past time)	It's over my head.	No, thanks.
Shame on you.	Bad idea.	Yes. (affirmative)	Ho Hum. (impatience)

Vocabulary 35

Gestures BINGO

Watch the teacher. The teacher will do a gesture. If you see the gesture on this board, mark the square. When you have four in a row, call out "BINGO!"

Good idea.	It's hot.	Yes, Sir!	Just a minute.
No. (negative)	Ho Hum. (impatience)	Me?	No, thanks.
Darn! (disappointment)	Shame on you.	I can't hear.	(money)
You're crazy.	Stop!	Come here.	Phew! (relief)

- ✂ -

Gestures BINGO

Watch the teacher. The teacher will do a gesture. If you see the gesture on this board, mark the square. When you have four in a row, call out "BINGO!"

Yes. (affirmative)	Just a minute.	It's cold.	Yesterday. (past time)
Bad idea.	Calm down!	It's over my head.	O.K.
YES! (excitement)	I don't know.	Good luck or Let's hope.	Look at that! (pointing)
Go away.	You're crazy.	Phew! (relief)	Be quiet!

Gestures BINGO

Watch the teacher. The teacher will do a gesture. If you see the gesture on this board, mark the square. When you have four in a row, call out "BINGO!"

Just a minute.	Yes. (affirmative)	Ho Hum. (impatience)	It's over my head.
Me?	No, thanks.	O.K.	Darn! (disappointment)
Phew! (relief)	Good luck or Let's hope.	Shame on you.	Look at that! (pointing)
Be quiet!	I can't hear.	(money)	I don't know.

------------------------------✂------------------------------

Gestures BINGO

Watch the teacher. The teacher will do a gesture. If you see the gesture on this board, mark the square. When you have four in a row, call out "BINGO!"

It's hot.	Yes, Sir!	No. (negative)	Good luck or Let's hope.
Look at that! (pointing)	You're crazy.	Go away.	Good idea.
Calm down!	Bad idea.	Yesterday. (past time)	YES! (excitement)
Come here.	No, thanks.	It's cold.	Stop!

Vocabulary 37

Gestures BINGO

Watch the teacher. The teacher will do a gesture. If you see the gesture on this board, mark the square. When you have four in a row, call out "BINGO!"

Me?	Ho Hum. (impatience)	No. (negative)	Yes, Sir!
It's hot.	Bad idea.	Calm down!	O.K.
Darn! (disappointment)	Good luck or Let's hope.	Look at that! (pointing)	I can't hear.
(money)	Stop!	Come here.	It's over my head.

- ✂ -

Gestures BINGO

Watch the teacher. The teacher will do a gesture. If you see the gesture on this board, mark the square. When you have four in a row, call out "BINGO!"

No, thanks.	YES! (excitement)	PHEW! (relief)	Shame on you.
Be quiet!	I don't know.	You're crazy.	Go away.
It's over my head.	Yes. (affirmative)	Just a minute.	It's cold.
Yesterday. (past time)	Good idea!	O.K.	(money)

Classroom BINGO

This game is used to expand students' knowledge of idioms and gives students the opportunity to talk to native speakers.

The BINGO Board
There is one board for this game. Every student should get BINGO at the same time.

The Cards
Before class, the teacher should photocopy and cut apart the cards on the next page. The teacher can glue each rectangle to an index card to make a permanent set.

The Procedure
❸ ❹ The teacher makes a copy of the board for each student. As homework, the students are responsible for finding out the meanings of the 25 idioms on the board before the game is played. They should ask native speakers on campus or in the community to help them. On the day that the game is played, the teacher mixes up the cards and places them face down on the table. The teacher draws the top card from the stack and reads the definitions. The students look at their boards and mark the appropriate square. When a student has marked five squares in a row (horizontally, vertically or diagonally), they should call out "BINGO!" If the students have done their homework, they should all call out "BINGO!" at the same time. The teacher should keep track of the words called by marking their own board. If no one calls out "BINGO!," when, in fact, the teacher sees that there are five in a row, the teacher should stop to review the definitions read. After the game ends, any discrepancies between native speaker definitions can be discussed.

Tips for Student Surveys
Before sending students out to interview native speakers, make sure that they are prepared.

• Teach the students how to politely interrupt people and how to introduce themselves and their task. For example, they can say, "Excuse me. I'm an English language student doing a survey for my English class. May I ask you a question?" Role-play this situation in class several times. Take the role of the native speaker. Be cooperative one time, but uncooperative the next (e.g., you can pretend that you're in a hurry). Tell the students to say "Thank you" or "Thanks anyway." Be sure that the students ask you the question orally instead of merely showing you their bingo board.

• As a class, practice the pronunciation of all the questions or clues.

• For low-level classes, consider sending the students out of the classroom in pairs.

• Make sure that the students do not all go to the same area to survey native speakers. Plan in advance where you will send each student or pair of students.

Vocabulary 39

Classroom BINGO	Instructions: Read the definitions. Students mark their boards.	This means to not go to a class one day. *Cut class*
This means to get started studying hard. *Hit the books*	This is an extremely difficult exam. *A killer exam*	This student is the teacher's favorite student. *The teacher's pet*
This means to fail all courses and be expelled from a school. *Flunk out of school*	This is a test given if a student is absent on the day *A make-up test*	This is the slang name for an athlete. *A jock*
This means to pass a course with no problems at all. *To breeze through a course*	This means that all a student's grades for a semester are "A." *Straight A's*	This means to officially stop attending a class. *Drop a class*
This means to get the lowest possible passing grade. *Pass by the skin of your teeth*	This means that a student cannot remember an answer to a question. *Draw a blank*	This means to memorize something (a poem, a list of verbs, etc.). *Learn by heart*
This means to do very poorly on a test. *Bomb a test*	This is a surprise quiz. *A pop quiz*	This student is usually in trouble for not being very serious in class (always making jokes). *The class clown*
This means to do extremely well on a test. *Ace a test*	This is the list of students in a school who get good grades in a given semester. *Honor roll*	This is the slang name for a very smart student. *A brain*
This means to stay up all night studying for a test. *Pull an all-nighter*	This means that the student is ranked #1 in the class. *At the head of the class*	This is a small piece of paper with test answers on it, used for cheating. *A cheat sheet*
This is a person who leaves school before graduating. *A dropout*	This means to hand something in at the last possible minute. *Hand something in under the wire*	This means that the teacher does not have time to assign more work because the class is over, and the students are "free." *Saved by the bell*

Reproducible for classroom use. Copyright © 2001 Nina Ito and Anne Berry.

Classroom BINGO

FOR HOMEWORK—Find out the meanings of the 25 idioms on this board. Ask native speakers to help you. Write the meanings in the squares.

IN CLASS—Listen to the teacher. The teacher will read a definition of an idiom. Mark an appropriate expression on the board. When you have five in a row, call out "BINGO!"

Cut class	Hit the books	A killer exam	The teacher's pet	Flunk out of school
A make-up test	A jock	To breeze through a course	Straight A's	Drop a class
Pass by the skin of your teeth	Draw a blank	Learn by heart	Bomb a test	A pop quiz
The class clown	Ace a test	The honor roll	A brain	Pull an all-nighter
At the head of the class	A cheat sheet	A dropout	Hand something in under the wire	Saved by the bell

Vocabulary 41

"Sink or Swim" BINGO

(Collocations and Idioms)

This game is used to expand students' colloquial vocabulary and give students the opportunity to talk to native speakers.

The BINGO Board
There is one board for this game. Every student should get BINGO at the same time.

The Cards
Before class, the teacher should photocopy and cut apart the cards on the next page. The teacher can glue each rectangle to an index card to make a permanent set.

The Procedure
❸ The teacher makes a copy of the board for each student. As a homework assignment, the students are responsible for finding out the meanings of the 25 binomials on the board before playing the game. They should ask native speakers on campus or in the community to help them. On the day that the game is played, the teacher mixes up the cards and places them face down on the table. The teacher draws the top card from the stack and reads the definitions. The students look at their boards and mark the appropriate square. When a student has marked five squares in a row (horizontally, vertically or diagonally), they should call out "BINGO!" If the students have done their homework, they should all call out "BINGO!" at the same time. The teacher should keep track of the words called by marking his or her own board. If no one calls out "BINGO!," when, in fact, the teacher sees that there are five in a row, the teacher should stop to review the definitions read. After the game ends, any discrepancies between native speaker definitions can be discussed.

Tips for Student Surveys
Before sending the students out to interview native speakers, make sure that they are prepared.

- Teach students how to politely interrupt people and how to introduce themselves and their task. For example, they can say, "Excuse me. I'm an English language student doing a survey for my English class. May I ask you a question?" Role-play this situation in class several times. Take the role of the native speaker. Be cooperative one time, but uncooperative the next (e.g., you can pretend that you're in a hurry). Tell the students to say "Thank you" or "Thanks anyway." Be sure that the students ask you the question orally instead of merely showing you their bingo board.

- As a class, practice the pronunciation of all the questions or clues.

- For low-level classes, consider sending the students out of the classroom in pairs.

- Make sure that the students do not all go to the same area to survey native speakers. Plan in advance where you will send each student or pair of students.

Alphabet BINGO

These games review the correct pronunciation of the names of the letters of the alphabet. (Note: Twenty-five letters fit on the board, and one letter is used as an example. In this way, all twenty-six letters of the alphabet can be practiced.)

The BINGO Board
There is one board for this game. Every student should get BINGO at the same time.

The Cards
Before class, the teacher should photocopy the board. To make a permanent set of cards, the teacher can glue the photocopy to a piece of cardboard and then cut the squares apart.

The Procedure
❶❷ Game 1: The teacher mixes up the cards and places them face down on the table. The teacher draws the top card from the stack and reads the letter. For example, if the teacher draws the card that says "B/b," the teacher says "bee". The students listen to the teacher, then look at their boards and mark the letter they heard. If the students know the correct name of each letter, they should all call out "BINGO!" at the same time. The teacher should keep track of the letters called by marking their own board. If no one calls out "BINGO!" when, in fact, the teacher sees that there are five in a row, the teacher should stop to review the letters called.

❶❷ Game 2: See Game 1, except that students take turns being the caller. If the caller has said the letters correctly, all of the other students should call out "BINGO!" at the same time. If they don't, the caller should review all the letters they called, repeating the correct pronunciation with the help of the teacher. Students can play in small groups or pairs.

Note
The vowels *a, e, i* are especially tricky, and you might want to be sure that you include them near the top of your stack.

Alphabet *BINGO*

Listen to the teacher. Mark the square with the letter you hear.
When you have five in a row, call out "BINGO!"

Example: The teacher says, "Double U".
You mark the square that says W/w.

W/w

Y/y	O/o	K/k	H/h	D/d
P/p	T/t	G/g	N/n	U/u
M/m	J/j	E/e	F/f	Z/z
A/a	R/r	B/b	S/s	Q/q
X/x	V/v	C/c	I/i	L/l

"I Can" / "I Can't" BINGO

(Reduced Stress)

These games practice recognition and production of stress patterns and vowel reduction.

The BINGO Board
There is one board for this game. Every student should get BINGO at the same time.

The Cards
Before class, the teacher should photocopy and cut apart the cards on the next page. The teacher can glue each rectangle to an index card to make a permanent set.

The Procedure
❶ ❷ Game 1: The teacher mixes up the cards and places them face down on the table. The teacher draws the top card from the stack and reads the sentence being careful to stress the sentence appropriately. ("Can" in the affirmative is normally reduced - /kən/, while "can't", the negative, always carries stress - /kænt/.) The students listen to the teacher, then look at their boards and mark the correct square. If the students have understood the teacher's pronunciation, they should all call out "BINGO!" at the same time. The teacher should keep track of the words called by marking their own board. If no one calls out "BINGO!", when, in fact, the teacher sees that there are five in a row, they should stop to review the sentences, emphasizing the correct stress.

❷ ❸ Game 2: See Game 1, except that students take turns being the caller. If the caller has pronounced the sentences correctly, all of the other students should call out "BINGO!" at the same time. If they don't, the caller should review all the sentences with the help of the teacher. Students can play in small groups or pairs.

I can play the piano very well.	I can't play the piano very well.	I can type fast.	I can't type fast.
I can understand that.	I can't understand that.	I can play the guitar.	I can't play the guitar.
I can go out late at night.	I can't go out late at night.	I can ski.	I can't ski.
I can sing the high notes.	I can't sing the high notes.	I can swim for an hour.	I can't swim for an hour.
I can paint.	I can't paint.	I can drive.	I can't drive.
I can cook.	I can't cook.	I can sleep during the day.	I can't sleep during the day.

Reproducible for classroom use. Copyright © 2001 Nina Ito and Anne Berry.

"I Can" / "I Can't" BINGO

Listen to the teacher.

If the teacher <u>can</u> do the activity, mark the open square.

If the teacher <u>can't</u> do the activity, mark the X-ed square.

When you have five in a row, call out "BINGO!"

Pronunciation BINGO Games

The BINGO Board
There is one board for these games. Every student should get BINGO at the same time.

The Cards
Before class, the teacher should photocopy the board to cut apart. To make a permanent set of cards, the teacher can glue the photocopy to a piece of cardboard before cutting the squares apart.

The Procedure
These games work well as part of a unit on the contrastive phonemes.

❶ ❷ Game 1: This variation practices phoneme recognition. The teacher mixes up the cards and places them face down on the table. The teacher draws the top card from the stack and reads the word, being careful to emphasize the target sound. The students listen and watch the teacher, then look at their boards and mark the word they heard. If the students have understood the teacher's pronunciation, they should all call out "BINGO!" at the same time. The teacher should keep track of the words called by marking their own board. If no one calls out "BINGO!", when, in fact, the teacher sees that there are five in a row, they should stop to review the words called. The game can be repeated to familiarize students with the target sounds in context and with the mouth positions.

After a few games, the teacher can shield their mouth with a piece of paper so that students must rely on what they hear, rather than the mouth position they see.

❷ ❸ ❹ Game 2: This variation practices phoneme production. See Game 1, except that students take turns being the caller. If the caller has pronounced the words correctly, all of the other students should call out "BINGO!" at the same time. If they don't, the caller should review all the words, repeating the unclear words with the help of the teacher. The students can play in small groups or pairs.

Notes
Pronounce "calves" as /kævs/.
As there are 25 squares in each board, one square does not have a contrasting paired sound. The non-contrastive sound is in the middle square.

Reproducible for classroom use. Copyright © 2001 Nina Ito and Anne Berry.

/b/ and /v/ BINGO

Listen to the teacher. Mark the square with the word you hear. When you have five in a row, call out "BINGO!"

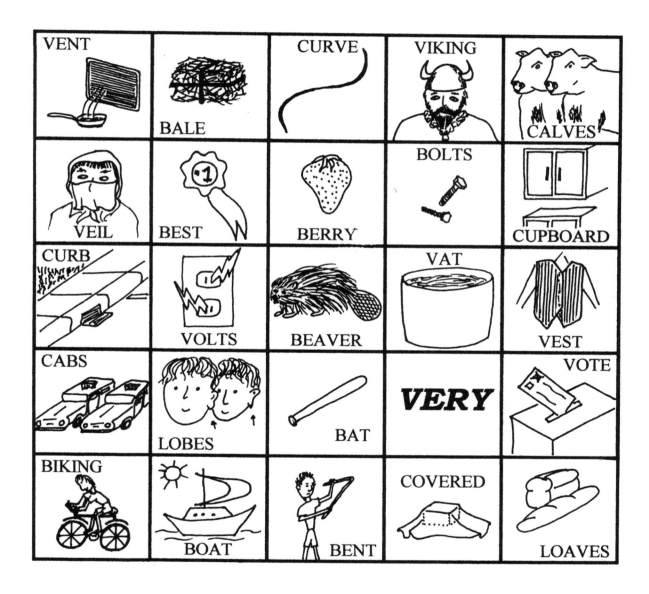

Pronunciation   53

/d/ and /ð/ BINGO

Listen to the teacher. Mark the square with the word you hear. When you have five in a row, call out "BINGO!"

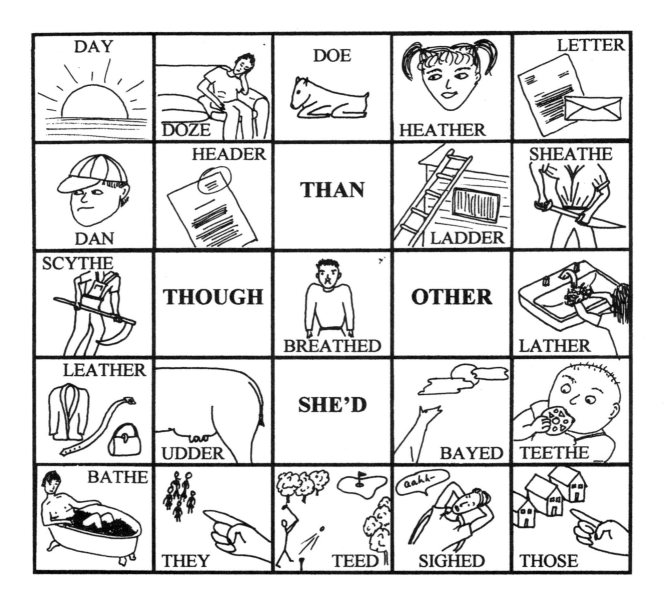

Reproducible for classroom use. Copyright © 2001 Nina Ito and Anne Berry.

/l/ and /r/ BINGO

Listen to the teacher. Mark the square with the word you hear. When you have five in a row, call out "BINGO!"

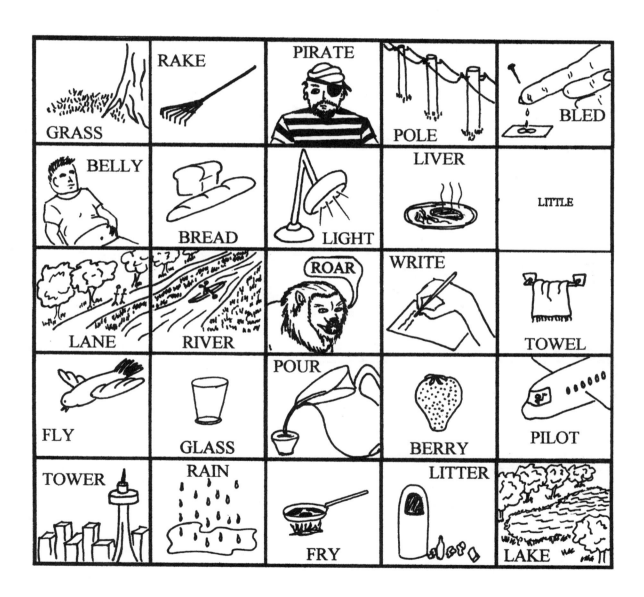

Pronunciation   55

/p/ and /f/ BINGO

Listen to the teacher. Mark the square with the word you hear. When you have five in a row, call out "BINGO!"

Reproducible for classroom use. Copyright © 2001 Nina Ito and Anne Berry.

/s/ and /θ/ BINGO

Listen to the teacher. Mark the square with the word you hear. When you have five in a row, call out "BINGO!"

Pronunciation 57

/æ/, /ʌ/ and /a/ BINGO

Listen to the teacher. Mark the square with the word you hear. When you have five in a row, call out "BINGO!"

Reproducible for classroom use. Copyright © 2001 Nina Ito and Anne Berry.

/i/ and /iy/ BINGO

Listen to the teacher. Mark the square with the word you hear. When you have five in a row, call out "BINGO!"

"In and Out" BINGO
(Prepositions)

This game tests students' understanding of prepositions of location.

The BINGO Boards
There are eight boards for this game. The students may play individually or in pairs. If there are more than 16 students in the class, extra boards may be photocopied. In this case, several students should get BINGO at the same time.

The Cards
Before class, the teacher should photocopy and cut apart the cards below. The teacher can glue each rectangle to an index card to make a permanent set.

The Procedure
❶ The students read the instructions and begin by writing one appropriate preposition in each square. Note: In some cases, there is more than one possible answer. For example, in the square where the ball is in front of the box, a student could write "near". The teacher mixes up the cards and places them face down on the table. The teacher draws the top card from the stack and reads the sentence. The students listen for the preposition. They look at their boards, and if they see that preposition, they mark the appropriate square. When a student has marked four squares in a row (horizontally, vertically or diagonally), they should call out "BINGO!" To confirm the win, the student tells the class which four they have in a row while the teacher verifies that these are correct.

"In and Out" BINGO (Prepositions)	The ball is above the box.	The ball is across from the box.	The balls are around the box.
The ball is behind the box.	The ball is beside the box.	The ball is between the boxes.	The ball is close to the box.
The ball is under the box.	The ball is far from the box.	The ball is in the box.	The ball is in front of the box.
The ball is in the corner of the box.	The ball is near the box.	The ball is next to the box.	The ball is on the box.
The ball is moving over the box.	The ball is moving through the box.	The ball is moving toward the box.	The ball is moving away from the box.

"In and Out" BINGO

Write a preposition that describes the position of the ball in each square. *(above, across from, around, away from, behind, beside, between, close to, far from, in, in front of, in the corner of, near, next to, on, over, through, toward, under)*

For example:

*The ball is **above** the box.*

*The ball is moving **toward** the box.*

Listen to the teacher. Mark the square with the preposition you hear. When you have four in a row, call out "BINGO!"

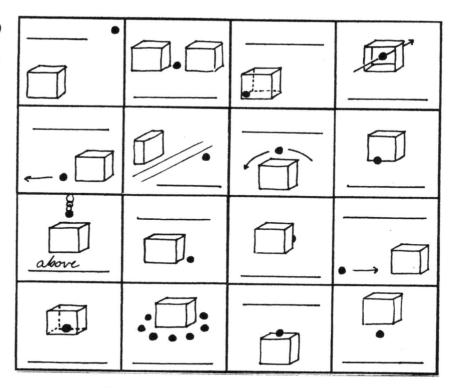

------------------------------✂------------------------------

"In and Out" BINGO

Write a preposition that describes the position of the ball in each square. *(above, across from, around, away from, behind, beside, between, close to, far from, in, in front of, in the corner of, near, next to, on, over, through, toward, under)*

For example:

*The ball is **above** the box.*

*The ball is moving **toward** the box.*

Listen to the teacher. Mark the square with the preposition you hear. When you have four in a row, call out "BINGO!"

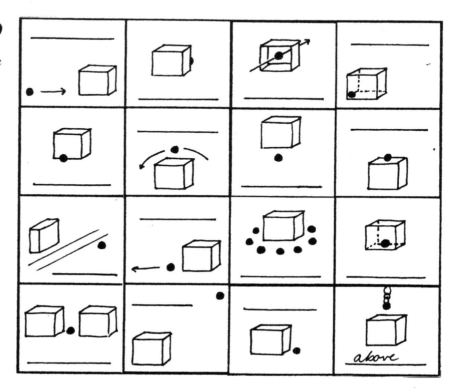

"In and Out" BINGO

Write a preposition that describes the position of the ball in each square. *(above, across from, around, away from, behind, beside, between, close to, far from, in, in front of, in the corner of, near, next to, on, over, through, toward, under)*

For example:

*The ball is **above** the box.*

*The ball is moving **toward** the box.*

Listen to the teacher. Mark the square with the preposition you hear. When you have four in a row, call out "BINGO!"

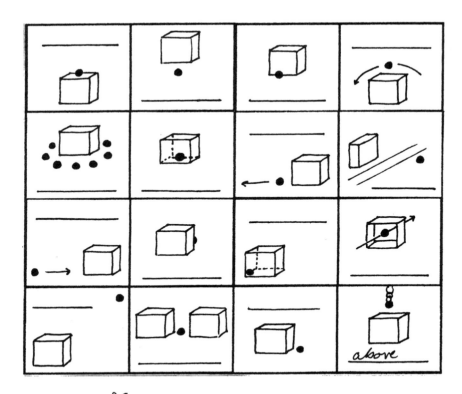

---✂---

"In and Out" BINGO

Write a preposition that describes the position of the ball in each square. *(above, across from, around, away from, behind, beside, between, close to, far from, in, in front of, in the corner of, near, next to, on, over, through, toward, under)*

For example:

*The ball is **above** the box.*

*The ball is moving **toward** the box.*

Listen to the teacher. Mark the square with the preposition you hear. When you have four in a row, call out "BINGO!"

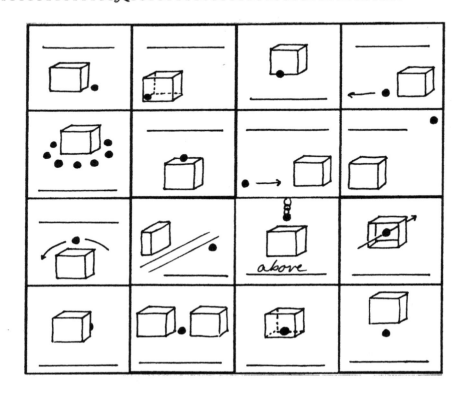

"In and Out" BINGO

Write a preposition that describes the position of the ball in each square. *(above, across from, around, away from, behind, beside, between, close to, far from, in, in front of, in the corner of, near, next to, on, over, through, toward, under)*

For example:

   *The ball is **above** the box.*

   *The ball is moving **toward** the box.*

Listen to the teacher. Mark the square with the preposition you hear. When you have four in a row, call out "BINGO!"

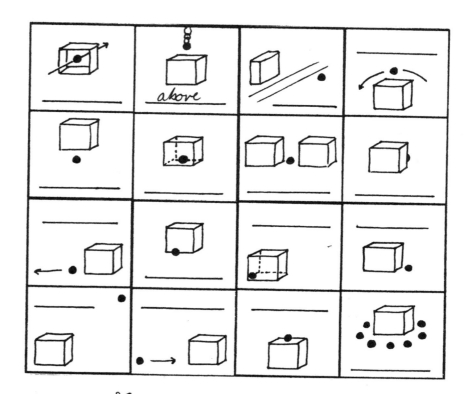

- ✂ -

"In and Out" BINGO

Write a preposition that describes the position of the ball in each square. *(above, across from, around, away from, behind, beside, between, close to, far from, in, in front of, in the corner of, near, next to, on, over, through, toward, under)*

For example:

   *The ball is **above** the box.*

   *The ball is moving **toward** the box.*

Listen to the teacher. Mark the square with the preposition you hear. When you have four in a row, call out "BINGO!"

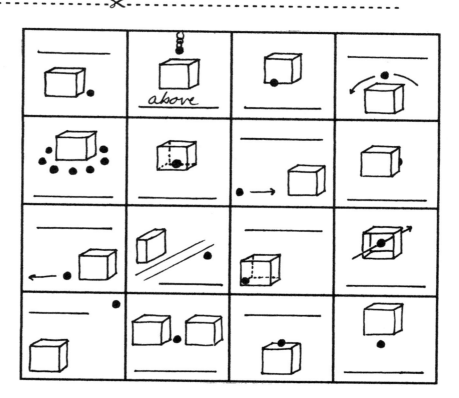

Grammar   63

"In and Out" BINGO

Write a preposition that describes the
position of the ball in each square.
*(above, across from, around, away
from, behind, beside, between,
close to, far from, in, in front of, in
the corner of, near, next to, on,
over, through, toward, under)*

For example:

> *The ball is **above** the box.*

> *The ball is moving **toward** the box.*

Listen to the teacher. Mark the
square with the preposition you
hear. When you have four in a row,
call out "BINGO!"

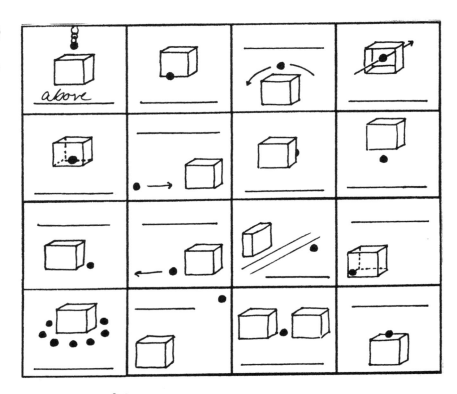

- ✂ -

"In and Out" BINGO

Write a preposition that describes the
position of the ball in each square.
*(above, across from, around, away
from, behind, beside, between,
close to, far from, in, in front of, in
the corner of, near, next to, on,
over, through, toward, under)*

For example:

> *The ball is **above** the box.*

> *The ball is moving **toward** the box.*

Listen to the teacher. Mark the
square with the preposition you
hear. When you have four in a row,
call out "BINGO!"

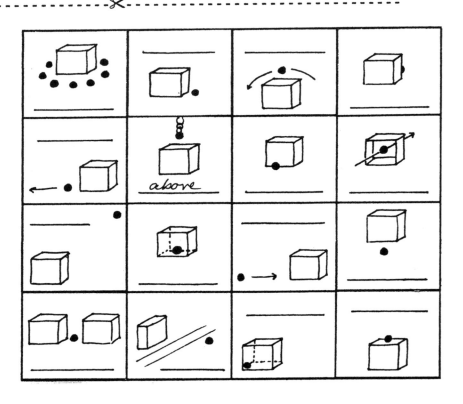

"Go, Went, Gone" BINGO

(Past Participles)

This game tests students' knowledge of irregular past participles.

The BINGO Board

There is one board for this game. Students who strategize will get BINGO first.

The Cards

Before class, the teacher should photocopy and cut apart the cards below and on the next page. The teacher can glue each rectangle to an index card to make a permanent set.

The Procedure

❶ The teacher mixes up the cards and places them face down on the table. The teacher draws the top card from the stack and reads the present and past tenses. The student may write the past participle in any square that already has the first letter of the answer. When a student has written a participle in five squares in a row (horizontally, vertically or diagonally), they should call out "BINGO!" To confirm the win, the student tells the class which five they have in a row and spells the words out loud while the teacher verifies that these are correct and spelled correctly. Note: The center square is a "free space."

Begin, began, … *begun*	Bite, bit, … *bitten*	Break, broke, … *broken*
Choose, chose, … *chosen*	Come, came, … *come*	Cost, cost, … *cost*
Cut, cut, … *cut*	Do, did, … *done*	Drink, drank, … *drunk*
Drive, drove, … *driven*	Eat, ate, … *eaten*	Fall, fell, … *fallen*
Fly, flew, … *flown*	Forget, forgot, … *forgotten*	Freeze, froze, … *frozen*

Get, got, ... *gotten (got)*	Give, gave, ... *given*	Go, went, ... *gone*
Hide, hid, ... *hidden*	Hit, hit, ... *hit*	Hurt, hurt, ... *hurt*
Know, knew, ... *known*	Read, read, ... *read*	Ride, rode, ... *ridden*
Ring, rang, ... *rung*	Rise, rose, ... *risen*	Run, ran, ... *run*
See, saw, ... *seen*	Show, showed, ... *shown (showed)*	Sing, sang, ... *sung*
Speak, spoke, ... *spoken*	Steal, stole, ... *stolen*	Swim, swam, ... *swum*
Take, took, ... *taken*	Tear, tore, ... *torn*	Throw, threw, ... *thrown*
Wake, woke, ... *woken*	Wear, wore, ... *worn*	Write, wrote, ... *written*

"Go, Went, Gone" BINGO

Listen to the teacher. The teacher will say the <u>present tense</u> and <u>past tense</u> of a verb. Write the <u>past participle</u> of the verb in a square that already has the first letter of the answer. When you have five in a row, call out "BINGO!" You may **not** change an answer from one box to another. Be sure to spell the words correctly!

t_____	k_____	s_____	c_____	w_____
g_____	r_____	b_____	h_____	d_____
w_____	h_____	**PAST PARTICIPLES**	s_____	r_____
s_____	c_____	t_____	f_____	e_____
d_____	l_____	f_____	g_____	b_____

Grammar 67

"What Did You Do?" BINGO

(Imperative/Past Tense)

This game tests students' knowledge of past tense verbs.

The BINGO Board

There is one board for this game. Students who strategize will get BINGO first.

The Procedure

❷ The teacher makes one copy of the board, then personalizes the game by filling in the remaining four squares with imperative sentences. Verbs that have *regular* or *irregular* past tense forms may be used. Ideas for filling in the squares include having students:

* use something specific inside their classroom.

* do something outside, yet near the classroom.

* interview a particular person in the class or near the classroom.

The teacher makes a copy of the board for each student. The students read the instructions at the top of the page and begin. Each student should choose a row (horizontal, vertical or diagonal) that can be done easily and quickly. While the students are working, the teacher circulates to monitor the activities. When a student has completed a row, they should fill in the exercise below the board and then call out "BINGO!" To confirm the win, the teacher asks, "What did you do?", and the student reads the four sentences out loud while the teacher verifies that they are correct and logical. The game can continue so that other students can get BINGO and read their sentences.

"What Did You Do?" BINGO

Choose one row (horizontal, vertical or diagonal). **Do** all four tasks.

Write a <u>funny</u> sentence on the board.	Get the signature of a student whose birthday is in the same month as yours		Give some advice to the teacher about the amount of homework in the class.
	Draw a picture of the teacher's face.	Borrow $1 from a classmate.	Hang one of your shoes in a funny place in the classroom.
Take a break! Relax for 2 minutes.		Find out who the youngest student in the class is.	Speak to a classmate for one minute about your favorite hobby.
Teach two students how to say "Thank you" in your native language.	Make a birthday card on a sheet of notebook paper.	Run around the classroom three times. Yell "I love English" as you pass the door.	

What did you do? Write the four **past tense** sentences here.

1. _____

2. _____

3. _____

4. _____

When you are finished, call out "BINGO!"

"So…" / "Neither…" BINGO *(Rejoinders)*

This game tests students' knowledge of the use of rejoinders.

The BINGO Boards
There are eight boards for this game. The students may play individually or in pairs. If there are more than 16 students in the class, extra boards may be photocopied. In this case, several students should get BINGO at the same time.

The Cards
Before class, the teacher should photocopy and cut apart the cards below. The teacher can glue each rectangle to an index card to make a permanent set.

The Procedure
❷ The teacher mixes up the cards and places them face down on the table. The teacher draws the top card from the stack and reads the sentence. The students look at their boards, and if they have the correct rejoinder, they mark the appropriate square. When a student has marked four squares in a row (horizontally, vertically or diagonally), they should call out "BINGO!" To confirm the win, the student tells the class which four they have in a row while the teacher verifies that these are correct.

"SO…" / "NEITHER…" BINGO (Rejoinders)	I need to study more. *So do I.*	Chen doesn't believe in UFOs. *Neither do most people.*
Aki bought a new car last month. *So did Manuel.*	He didn't look very tired. *Neither did she.*	We're not very hungry. *Neither am I.*
Diane's a twin. *So is Daniel.*	Olga was so happy yesterday. *So was Karen.*	I wasn't born in Los Angeles. *Neither were we.*
Mohammed will have a test on Monday. *So will Abdul.*	Joe won't be able to come to the party. *Neither will Bob.*	María can sing very well. *So can Kanako.*
Jean-Claude can't play golf at all. *Neither can Renato.*	Children should eat more vegetables. *So should adults.*	She shouldn't smoke so much. *Neither should her husband.*
We'd like to go to Paris. *So would we.*	I wouldn't want to be a lawyer. *Neither would I.*	I could use more money. *So could everyone.*
José couldn't stop laughing! *Neither could I.*	My parents have been to New York City twice. *So have mine.*	Frank has never tried sushi. *Neither have I.*

Reproducible for classroom use. Copyright © 2001 Nina Ito and Anne Berry.

"So..." / "Neither..." BINGO

Listen to the teacher. If you see the answer on this board, mark the square. When you have four in a row, call out "BINGO!"

So should adults.	So is Daniel.	Neither did she.	Neither will Bob.
So can Kanako.	Neither could I.	Neither am I.	So could everyone.
Neither do most people.	So was Karen.	So have mine.	Neither were we.
So will Abdul.	Neither can Renato.	Neither have I.	So would we.

---✂---

"So..." / "Neither..." BINGO

Listen to the teacher. If you see the answer on this board, mark the square. When you have four in a row, call out "BINGO!"

Neither can Renato.	So could everyone.	Neither were we.	Neither could I.
So can Kanako.	So do I.	So would we.	Neither will Bob.
So should adults.	So did Manuel.	Neither did she.	So will Abdul.
So was Karen.	Neither should her husband.	Neither do most people.	Neither have I.

"So…" / "Neither…" BINGO

Listen to the teacher. If you see the answer on this board, mark the square. When you have four in a row, call out "BINGO!"

So can Kanako.	So have mine.	So do I.	Neither do most people.
Neither can Renato.	Neither could I.	So will Abdul.	Neither should her husband.
So would we.	So should adults.	Neither will Bob.	Neither am I.
So is Daniel.	Neither were we.	Neither would I.	So did Manuel.

- -✂- -

"So…" / "Neither…" BINGO

Listen to the teacher. If you see the answer on this board, mark the square. When you have four in a row, call out "BINGO!"

Neither can Renato.	So could everyone.	So do I.	Neither were we.
So did Manuel.	So is Daniel.	So have mine.	Neither will Bob.
Neither should her husband.	So would we.	Neither did she.	Neither have I.
Neither would I.	So was Karen.	Neither do most people.	So can Kanako.

"So..." / "Neither..." BINGO

Listen to the teacher. If you see the answer on this board, mark the square. When you have four in a row, call out "BINGO!"

So did Manuel.	So is Daniel.	Neither do most people.	Neither would I.
Neither have I.	Neither will Bob.	Neither am I.	Neither should her husband.
So was Karen.	So will Abdul.	So could everyone.	Neither can Renato.
Neither did she.	So can Kanako.	Neither could I.	So should adults.

- ✂ -

"So..." / "Neither..." BINGO

Listen to the teacher. If you see the answer on this board, mark the square. When you have four in a row, call out "BINGO!"

Neither have I.	So was Karen.	So did Manuel.	So could everyone.
So will Abdul.	Neither were we.	Neither would I.	So do I.
Neither did she.	So have mine.	Neither should her husband.	Neither could I.
Neither can Renato.	Neither am I.	So should adults.	So is Daniel.

Reproducible for classroom use. Copyright © 2001 Nina Ito and Anne Berry.   Grammar   73

"So..." / "Neither..." BINGO

Listen to the teacher. If you see the answer on this board, mark the square. When you have four in a row, call out "BINGO!"

So do I.	So could everyone.	Neither could I.	So would we.
Neither did she.	Neither am I.	So have mine.	So should adults.
So is Daniel.	Neither do most people.	Neither will Bob.	Neither can Renato.
Neither have I.	Neither should her husband.	So was Karen.	So will Abdul.

- ✄ -

"So..." / "Neither..." BINGO

Listen to the teacher. If you see the answer on this board, mark the square. When you have four in a row, call out "BINGO!"

Neither have I.	Neither could I.	So could everyone.	Neither am I.
So do I.	Neither did she.	Neither do most people.	Neither were we.
So was Karen.	Neither will Bob.	Neither should her husband.	So should adults.
So can Kanako.	So have mine.	Neither would I.	So would we.

Tag Question BINGO

This game tests students' knowledge of the use of tag questions.

The BINGO Boards

There are eight boards for this game. The students may play individually or in pairs. If there are more than 16 students in the class, extra boards may be photocopied. In this case, several students should get BINGO at the same time.

The Cards

Before class, the teacher should photocopy and cut apart the cards on the next page. The teacher can glue each rectangle to an index card to make a permanent set.

The Procedure

❷ The teacher mixes up the cards and places them face down on the table. The teacher draws the top card from the stack and reads the first part of the sentence. The students look at their boards, and if they have the correct tag question, they mark the appropriate square. When a student has marked four squares in a row (horizontally, vertically, or diagonally), they should call out "BINGO!" To confirm the win, the student tells the class which four they have in a row while the teacher verifies that these are correct.

Grammar   75

I'm speaking clearly *..., aren't I?*	You're Dr. Harper *..., aren't you?*	It's not unusual, *..., is it?*
She's not coming *..., is she?*	I wasn't lying *..., was I?*	John wasn't on time *..., was he?*
You were right *..., weren't you?*	I don't look sad *..., do I?*	He knows the answer *..., doesn't he?*
We didn't lose it *..., did we?*	It rained yesterday *..., didn't it?*	Bob won't buy a new car *..., will he?*
We'll see each other soon *..., won't we?*	I can have this one *..., can't I?*	It can't be true *..., can it?*
You couldn't climb that mountain *..., could you?*	Marta could drive you *..., couldn't she?*	We should be more careful *..., shouldn't we?*
They shouldn't do that *..., should they?*	You wouldn't want to live there *..., would you?*	They'd like to win *..., wouldn't they?*
You've got the money *..., haven't you?*	They haven't had much luck *..., have they?*	Your sister had been there before *..., hadn't she?*

Tag Question BINGO

Listen to the teacher. If you can complete the sentence with a tag question on this board, mark the square. When you have four in a row, call out "BINGO!"

..., could you?	..., aren't I?	..., can it?	..., is it?
..., is she?	..., haven't you?	..., did we?	..., should they?
..., can't I?	..., do I?	..., couldn't she?	..., hadn't she?
..., aren't you?	..., didn't it?	..., shouldn't we?	..., will he?

- ✄ -

Tag Question BINGO

Listen to the teacher. If you can complete the sentence with a tag question on this board, mark the square. When you have four in a row, call out "BINGO!"

..., is she?	..., did we?	..., doesn't he?	..., aren't I?
..., have they?	..., weren't you?	..., is it?	..., haven't you?
..., was he?	..., can't I?	..., hadn't she?	..., aren't you?
..., could you?	..., will he?	..., didn't it?	..., can it?

Grammar 77

Tag Question BINGO

Listen to the teacher. If you can complete the sentence with a tag question on this board, mark the square. When you have four in a row, call out "BINGO!"

..., won't we?	..., doesn't he?	..., do I?	..., was he?
..., can it?	..., aren't I?	..., wouldn't they?	..., didn't it?
..., haven't you?	..., weren't you?	..., should they?	..., would you?
..., could you?	..., was I?	..., have they?	..., can't I?

- ✂ -

Tag Question BINGO

Listen to the teacher. If you can complete the sentence with a tag question on this board, mark the square. When you have four in a row, call out "BINGO!"

..., hadn't she?	..., doesn't he?	..., have they?	..., is she?
..., aren't you?	..., was I?	..., won't we?	..., would you?
..., couldn't she?	..., shouldn't we?	..., is it?	..., wouldn't they?
..., was he?	..., will he?	..., weren't you?	..., did we?

Tag Question BINGO

Listen to the teacher. If you can complete the sentence with a tag question on this board, mark the square. When you have four in a row, call out "BINGO!"

..., *should they?*	..., *is she?*	..., *can't I?*	..., *didn't it?*
..., *aren't you?*	..., *did we?*	..., *couldn't she?*	..., *hadn't she?*
..., *weren't you?*	..., *doesn't he?*	..., *do I?*	..., *wouldn't they?*
..., *shouldn't we?*	..., *won't we?*	..., *is it?*	..., *will he?*

-----------------------------✄-----------------------------

Tag Question BINGO

Listen to the teacher. If you can complete the sentence with a tag question on this board, mark the square. When you have four in a row, call out "BINGO!"

..., *aren't you?*	..., *couldn't she?*	..., *will he?*	..., *would you?*
..., *should they?*	..., *can't I?*	..., *do I?*	..., *did we?*
..., *could you?*	..., *didn't it?*	..., *was I?*	..., *can it?*
..., *have they?*	..., *was he?*	..., *aren't I?*	..., *haven't you?*

Grammar   79

Tag Question BINGO

Listen to the teacher. If you can complete the sentence with a tag question on this board, mark the square. When you have four in a row, call out "BINGO!"

…, can it?	*…, was he?*	*…, haven't you?*	*…, shouldn't we?*
…, is it?	*…, wouldn't they?*	*…, should they?*	*…, was I?*
…, couldn't she?	*…, didn't it?*	*…, did we?*	*…, can't I?*
…, weren't you?	*…, will he?*	*…, do I?*	*…, aren't you?*

- ✂ -

Tag Question BINGO

Listen to the teacher. If you can complete the sentence with a tag question on this board, mark the square. When you have four in a row, call out "BINGO!"

…, weren't you?	*…, is it?*	*…, wouldn't they?*	*…, shouldn't we?*
…, doesn't he?	*…, haven't you?*	*…, can it?*	*…, was he?*
…, aren't I?	*…, hadn't she?*	*…, is she?*	*…, would you?*
…, have they?	*…, was I?*	*…, won't we?*	*…, could you?*

Reproducible for classroom use. Copyright © 2001 Nina Ito and Anne Berry.

Correct the Grammar BINGO

(Count/Non-Count Nouns)

These games teach and test count/non-count noun rules.

The BINGO Board
There is one board for this game.

The Procedure
❷ Game 1: The teacher makes a copy of the board for each pair of students. The students choose a row (horizontal, vertical, or diagonal) that they can correct. When a pair of students has completed five squares in a row, they should call out "BINGO!" To confirm the win, one student of the pair goes to the board to write the five corrected sentences. During this time, the other students continue to work on their sentences. If the five sentences are correct, the pair is declared the winner. If any of the sentences are incorrect, the student must sit down. The game then continues so that other students can get BINGO and check their answers.

❷ Game 2: See Game 1, except that students may consult a grammar textbook.

Answer Key

Row 1   What nice weather! (No "**a**")
We bought some **food** at that supermarket.
They've got **a lot of** money in the bank.
The T.V. news today **is** very depressing.
He knows a lot of **vocabulary**.

Row 2   Please give me some **advice**.
There **is** too much violence in movies nowadays.
Teenagers have a lot of **stuff** in their bedrooms.
How much homework do you have tonight? CORRECT
After I graduate, I'll look for work. (No "**a**")

Row 3   I need some **information** about New York City.
Most soldiers have courage. (No "**a**")
Fruit **is** good for you.
Those **children** always look happy.
How **long** have you lived here?

Row 4   There **is** too much traffic in this city!
You won't get a good job without **experience**.
She has beautiful hair. (No "**a**")
They need to buy some **furniture**.
She ate too **many** apples and got sick!

Row 5   How **many** letters did you receive?
That farmer owns a lot of sheep. CORRECT.
She wears too much **jewelry**.
I've got **a** headache.
There **is** a lot of **equipment** in this room.

Correct the Grammar BINGO

Work in pairs. Choose one row (horizontal, vertical, or diagonal). If the sentence has a grammar error, correct it. If the sentence is correct, circle it. When you have five correct sentences in a row, call out "BINGO!"

What a nice weather!	We bought some foods at that supermarket.	They've got much money in the bank.	The TV news today are very depressing.	He knows a lot of vocabularies
Please give me some advices.	There are too much violence in movies nowadays.	Teenagers have a lot of stuffs in their bedrooms.	How much homework do you have tonight?	After I graduate, I'll look for a work.
I need some informations about New York City.	Most soldiers have a courage.	Fruit are good for you.	Those childrens always look happy.	How long time have you lived here?
There are too much traffic in this city!	You won't get a good job without experiences.	She has a beautiful hair.	They need to buy some furnitures.	She ate too much apples and got sick.
How much letters did you receive?	That farmer owns a lot of sheep.	She wears too much jewelries.	I've got headache.	There is a lot of equipments in this room.

Question and Answer BINGO

This game tests students' knowledge of question words and yes/no questions.

The BINGO Boards

There are eight boards for this game. The students may play individually or in pairs. If there are more than 16 students in the class, extra boards may be photocopied. In this case, several students should get BINGO at the same time.

The Cards

Before class, the teacher should photocopy and cut apart the cards on the next page. The teacher can glue each rectangle to an index card to make a permanent set.

The Procedure

❶ ❷ The teacher mixes up the cards and places them face down on the table. The teacher draws the top card from the stack and reads the "answer." The students look at their boards, and if they have the appropriate question, they write the answer in the square. For example, if the teacher reads, "It's in January," the students write that answer in a square with "When is your birthday?" When a student has marked four squares in a row (horizontally, vertically, or diagonally), they should call out "BINGO!" To confirm the win, the student reads the four question and answer pairs out loud while the teacher verifies that they make sense.

Clues for Question and Answer Bingo

Yes, I do. *Do you use e-mail?*	Yes, I was. *Were you an active child?*	Yes, I am. *Are you thirsty?*
Yes, I can. *Can you swim?*	Yes, I will. *Will you graduate soon?*	Yes, I did. *Did you study hard?*
Yes, I would. *Would you like some coffee?*	I'm trying to relax. *What are you doing?*	Fine. *How are you?*
Six o'clock. *What time is it?*	It's in January. *When is your birthday?*	In the closet. *Where are the extra towels?*
It means "very big." *What does "huge" mean?*	Your father. *Who called?*	This one. *Which one do you want?*
Mine. *Whose car is that?*	Because it was on sale. *Why did you buy that dress?*	A surgeon. *What kind of doctor are you?*
Three hours. *How long does it last?*	It's 3,000 square feet. *How big is your house?*	He's 82. *How old is your grandfather?*
Not much. *How much money do you have?*	Two. *How many do you want?*	Perfectly. *How well do you speak English?*
As soon as possible. *How soon do you need it?*	Once a week. *How often do you eat out?*	93 million miles. *How far away is the sun?*

Question and Answer BINGO

Listen to the teacher. The teacher will say a short answer. If you see the question on this board, write the answer in the square. When you have four in a row, call out "BINGO!"

Would you like some coffee?	How old is your grandfather?	What are you doing?	How much money do you have?
When is your birthday?	How soon do you need it?	Which one do you want?	How long does it last?
Did you study hard?	Whose car is that?	How far away is the sun?	Do you use e-mail?
Who called?	Why did you buy that dress?	Where are the extra towels?	What time is it?

- ✁ -

Question and Answer BINGO

Listen to the teacher. The teacher will say a short answer. If you see the question on this board, write the answer in the square. When you have four in a row, call out "BINGO!"

What kind of doctor are you?	How old is your grandfather?	What are you doing?	Are you thirsty?
Whose car is that?	How well do you speak English?	Will you graduate soon?	When is your birthday?
Which one do you want?	What time is it?	Who called?	Do you use e-mail?
Were you an active child?	How are you?	Can you swim?	Where are the extra towels?

Grammar   85

Question and Answer BINGO

Listen to the teacher. The teacher will say a short answer. If you see the question on this board, write the answer in the square. When you have four in a row, call out "BINGO!"

How old is your grandfather?	What kind of doctor are you?	How often do you eat out?	How long does it last?
How soon do you need it?	Can you swim?	How much money do you have?	What does "huge" mean?
How many do you want?	Would you like some coffee?	Are you thirsty?	How far away is the sun?
How big is your house?	Where are the extra towels?	Do you use e-mail?	What time is it?

--------------------------------✂--------------------------------

Question and Answer BINGO

Listen to the teacher. The teacher will say a short answer. If you see the question on this board, write the answer in the square. When you have four in a row, call out "BINGO!"

Will you graduate soon?	What does "huge" mean?	What are you doing?	When is your birthday?
Which one do you want?	How are you?	How many do you want?	How often do you eat out?
Whose car is that?	Are you thirsty?	How well do you speak English?	Did you study hard?
How far away is the sun?	Who called?	Were you an active child?	Why did you buy that dress?

Question and Answer BINGO

Listen to the teacher. The teacher will say a short answer. If you see the question on this board, write the answer in the square. When you have four in a row, call out "BINGO!"

How much money do you have?	How often do you eat out?	Why is the sky blue?	How well do you speak English?
Will you graduate soon?	Would you like some coffee?	How many do you want?	Whose car is that?
What does "huge" mean?	Did you study hard?	What kind of doctor are you?	Are you thirsty?
What are you doing?	How old is your grandfather?	How big is your house?	How far away is the sun?

------------------------------✂------------------------------

Question and Answer BINGO

Listen to the teacher. The teacher will say a short answer. If you see the question on this board, write the answer in the square. When you have four in a row, call out "BINGO!"

Will you graduate soon?	When is your birthday?	Which one do you want?	How are you?
How long does it last?	How soon do you need it?	Can you swim?	How much money do you have?
How well do you speak English?	Why did you buy that dress?	Were you an active child?	Who called?
Do you use e-mail?	What time is it?	Where are the extra towels?	How big is your house?

Grammar 87

Question and Answer BINGO

Listen to the teacher. The teacher will say a short answer. If you see the question on this board, write the answer in the square. When you have four in a row, call out "BINGO!"

Do you use e-mail?	Who called?	What time is it?	Were you an active child?
Where are the extra towels?	Why did you buy that dress?	How big is your house?	How well do you speak English?
How far away is the sun?	Whose car is that?	Are you thirsty?	Did you study hard?
What kind of doctor are you?	How often do you eat out?	Would you like some coffee?	How many do you want?

- ✂ -

Question and Answer BINGO

Listen to the teacher. The teacher will say a short answer. If you see the question on this board, write the answer in the square. When you have four in a row, call out "BINGO!"

How long does it last?	How are you?	How soon do you need it?	Which one do you want?
When is your birthday?	Will you graduate soon?	What does "huge" mean?	What are you doing?
What kind of doctor are you?	Would you like some coffee?	Did you study hard?	How often do you eat out?
Can you swim?	How much money do you have?	How old is your grandfather?	How many do you want?

Celebrity BINGO
(Modals)

These games provide practice with modals.

The BINGO Board
There is one board for this game.

The Procedure

❸ Game 1: Before class, the teacher makes one copy of the board for each student and prepares a list of famous people. In class, the teacher says the name of a famous person, and then the teacher calls out the letter or number of a row. (Note: Horizontal rows are labeled A, B, C and D; vertical rows are labeled 1, 2, 3 and 4; diagonal rows are labeled X and Y.) The students must write four sentences, one with each modal in that row, about the famous person. The students should write each sentence in the appropriate square. For example, the teacher says the name of a film star, "Tom Showbiz," and then calls out "Row B". A student might write, "Tom Showbiz <u>may</u> get divorced soon," or "Tom Showbiz <u>can't</u> go out in public without being recognized," etc. When a student has written four sentences, they should call out "BINGO!" To confirm the win, the student reads the four sentences out loud while the teacher verifies that they are correct and logical. The game can continue so that other students can get BINGO and read their sentences.

❸ Game 2: See Game 1, except that, instead of famous people, the teacher says the names of students in the class. The class must use the modals in a given row to make sentences about the student whose name was called.

Celebrity BINGO

Listen to the teacher. The teacher will say the name of a famous person or a student in this class. Then the teacher will call out a number or letter. Write four sentences, one with each modal in that row, about that person. Use true information. When you are finished, call out "BINGO!"

X	1	2	3	4	Y
A	(mustn't)	(should)	(might not)	(will)	
B	(may)	(can't)	(must)	(doesn't have to)	
C	(can)	(has to)	(shouldn't)	(couldn't)	
D	(wouldn't)	(won't)	(ought to)	(might)	

Reproducible for classroom use. Copyright © 2001 Nina Ito and Anne Berry.

Gerund and Infinitive BINGO

This game tests students' knowledge of when to use an infinitive vs. when to use a gerund.

The Bingo Board
This game is played in pairs. There is one board for Student A and one board for Student B.

The Procedure
❸ ❹ The teacher makes a photocopy of one of the boards for each student—half get the board labeled "Student A" and half get the board labeled "Student B." The teacher instructs the pairs of students (Student A + Student B) to sit face to face, not side by side. The students read the instructions at the top of the page. The teacher clarifies the instructions if necessary. While the students are working, the teacher circulates to make sure the students understand how to play; however, the teacher should not correct any of the students' sentences at that time. When a student has completed a row (horizontally, vertically or diagonally), they should call out "BINGO!" To confirm the win, the student reads the five sentences out loud while the teacher verifies that they are grammatically correct. NOTE: Since there are several possible endings for most of the sentences, an answer key is not provided. The game can continue so that other students can get BINGO and read their sentences.

Gerund and Infinitive BINGO
Student A

Work with **Student B.** Sit face to face, not side by side. Begin by reading the *first part* of any sentence on the board. Student B will listen, then tell you an appropriate ending on their board. If you agree that the complete sentence is grammatically correct and logical, write the complete sentence in your square. Then, continue the game with Student B reading the first part of a sentence. When you have five complete sentences in a row, call out "BINGO!"

	I'd like...		She finished...	
...to arrive on time.		...watching baseball on TV.		...getting a cat.
My brother hates...		The teens suggested...		Keep...
	...to attend a university near her home.		...to keep it a secret.	
They can't wait...				The criminal refused...
	...eating a good breakfast.	...to study hard.	...smoking last year.	
The movie star appears...		He didn't mean...		Don't forget...
	...to buy my car.		...to feed your cat in the morning.	
	It began...		I miss...	
...skiing next week.		...committing that crime.		...buying a bigger car for ourselves.

Gerund and Infinitive BINGO
Student B

Work with **Student A**. Sit face to face, not side by side. Listen to Student A. Student A will read the first part of a sentence. Look on the board and choose an appropriate *ending*. Read the ending to Student A. If Student A agrees that the complete sentence is grammatically correct and logical, write the complete sentence in your square. Then, continue the game by reading the *first part* of any sentence on the board. When you have five complete sentences in a row, call out "BINGO!"

	You always remember...		My sister's going...	
...to know more about your past.		...to snow.		...driving so far to work.
We considered...		Please continue...		My father quit...
	...being with my family.		...to be younger than she really is.	
That man offered...				They'll discuss...
	...practicing your English.	...to break that expensive vase.	...writing a letter to her friend.	
Everyone agreed...		We won't deny...		She decided...
	...to turn off the lights.		...going to the dentist.	
	Doctors recommend...		I love...	
...to attend their friend's party.		...going to their favorite restaurant.		...to surrender.

Grammar Terms BINGO

This game serves as a comprehensive review of the terms often used in grammar texts .

The BINGO Board
There is one board for this game. Every student should get BINGO at the same time.

The Cards
Before class, the teacher should photocopy and cut apart the cards below. The teacher can glue each rectangle to an index card to make a permanent set.

The Procedure
❹ The teacher makes a copy of the board for each student. The teacher mixes up the cards and places them face down on the table. The teacher draws the top card from the stack and reads the grammar term. The students listen, then look at their boards and write the term in the square with the sentence that illustrates that point. When a student has four squares in a row (horizontally, vertically, or diagonally), they should call out "BINGO!" If the students have filled in the correct terms, they should all call out "BINGO" at the same time. The teacher should keep track of the terms called by marking their own board. If no one calls out "BINGO!", when the teacher sees that there are four in a row, they should stop to review the terms called. After the game ends, all the sentences on the board can be discussed.

Grammar Terms BINGO	**Instructions:** Read the grammar terms. Students write them in the appropriate squares.	SIMPLE PRESENT *I like this BINGO game.*
SIMPLE PAST *They went downtown yesterday.*	FUTURE *Will you graduate next year?*	PRESENT CONTINUOUS *I'm living with some friends until my new apartment is ready.*
PAST CONTINUOUS *What were you doing last night?*	FUTURE CONTINUOUS *When we move to San Diego, we'll be going to the beach regularly.*	PRESENT PERFECT *He's seen that film twice.*
PAST PERFECT *She'd been in London before.*	PRESENT PERFECT CONTINUOUS *I've been reading this novel for three weeks.*	PAST PERFECT CONTINUOUS *He'd been eating at that restaurant every Saturday before it closed.*
UNREAL PRESENT CONDITIONAL *If I had enough money, I'd buy a new car.*	UNREAL PAST CONDITIONAL *If she hadn't been in a hurry, she wouldn't have had an accident.*	REPORTED SPEECH *They said that they were hungry.*
TAG QUESTIONS *It's a nice day, isn't it?*	PASSIVE *That essay was written by the best student in the class.*	RELATIVE CLAUSE *The guy who is sitting over there is my boy friend.*

Grammar Terms BINGO

Work alone. In each square, write the grammar point (e.g. tense) that is underlined in the sentence. As an example, see the top left square.

Then listen to the teacher. The teacher will say a grammar point. Mark the square with the sentence that illustrates that grammar point. When you have four in a row, call out "BINGO!"

I <u>like</u> this BINGO game. *simple present*	He'<u>d been eating</u> at that restaurant every Saturday before it closed.	When we move to San Diego, we'<u>ll be going</u> to the beach regularly.	<u>If</u> I <u>had</u> enough money, I'<u>d buy</u> a new car.
<u>If</u> she <u>hadn't been</u> in a hurry, she <u>wouldn't have had</u> the accident.	It's a nice day, <u>isn't it?</u>	They <u>went</u> downtown yesterday.	The guy <u>who is sitting over there</u> is my boyfriend.
She'<u>d been</u> in London before.	<u>Will</u> you <u>graduate</u> next year?	I'<u>ve been reading</u> this novel for three weeks.	He'<u>s seen</u> that film twice.
I'<u>m living</u> with some friends until my new apartment is ready.	That essay <u>was written by</u> the best student in the class.	What <u>were</u> you <u>doing</u> last night?	<u>They said that they</u> were hungry.

Make a Sentence BINGO
(Sentence Formation)

This game helps students review vocabulary and practice writing.

The Board
There is one board for this game. Eight of the squares are already filled in. Below the board there is a list of fifteen words (A). First the students choose nine of these words (pronouns, verbs, nouns, etc.) and write them in any nine empty squares on the board. Then they write eight other vocabulary items they have recently learned in the blanks (*a* to *h*) in section B. Finally, the students write these eight words in all the empty squares on the board. In this way, every student has a different board.

The Procedure
❷ ❸ The teacher makes one copy of the board, then personalizes the game by filling in Part B with eight words from a recent lesson. Then the teacher makes a copy for each student or pair of students. In class, the teacher helps the students follow the instructions for filling in the board. When the students are ready, the teacher calls out the letter or number of a row. (Note: Horizontal rows are labeled A, B, C, D and E; vertical rows are labeled 1, 2, 3, 4 and 5; diagonal rows are labeled X and Y.) The students must include all five words in that row in an original sentence. When a student writes a complete sentence, they should call out "BINGO!" To confirm the win, the student reads the sentence out loud while the teacher decides whether it's correct. The game can continue so that other students can get BINGO and read their sentences.

Make a Sentence BINGO

	1	2	3	4	5
A			the		yet
B	and				
C		or			a
D			but		
E	I			so	

X ... Y

Instructions: A. Choose NINE of these fifteen words and write them in any of the empty squares:

he	she	we	it	house
have	ask	visit	buy	someone
difficult	fun	lovely	pencil	interesting

B. Write these EIGHT words in any of the empty squares:

a. _____   b. _____   c. _____   d. _____
e. _____   f. _____   g. _____   h. _____

C. Listen to the teacher. The teacher will call out a number or letter. Write ONE sentence that includes all five words in that row. When you are finished, call out "BINGO!" Then read your sentence to the class.

"Bigger, Better" BINGO
(Comparisons)

These games provide practice with comparative structures.

The BINGO Board
There is one board for this game. Students who strategize will get BINGO first.

The Cards
Before class, the teacher should photocopy and cut apart the cards on the next page. There are extra cards in case the teachers wants to add other words that are appropriate for these comparisons. The teacher can glue each rectangle to an index card to make a permanent set. Note: For Game 2, the teacher needs to prepare more than one set of cards.

The Procedure
❷ Game 1: The teacher makes a copy of the board for each student. The teacher mixes up the cards and places them face down on the table. The teacher draws the top card from the stack and reads the word. The students look at their boards and choose a square with a word that can be compared to the word that was read. Each student writes a sentence in that square that compares the two objects. For example, the teacher reads, "a diamond ring". One student might write, "My diamond ring is more expensive than my bicycle." Another student might write, "My diamond ring is more elegant than my watch." Another student might write, "My diamond ring is smaller than my refrigerator." Any correct and logical sentence can be used to mark that square. When a student has written sentences in four squares in a row (horizontally, vertically or diagonally), they should call out "BINGO!" To confirm the win, the student reads the four sentences out loud while the teacher verifies that they are correct and logical. The game can continue so that other students can get BINGO and read their sentences.

❸ Game 2: See Game 1, except that students sit in groups of four. Each student has a board, and each group has a stack of cards. Students take turns drawing and reading cards from the stack. When a student calls out "BINGO!", the group judges the correctness of the sentences with the help of the teacher.

Reproducible for classroom use. Copyright © 2001 Nina Ito and Anne Berry.

"Bigger, Better" BINGO	a Rolls Royce	a motorcycle	a truck
a bed	a sofa	a helicopter	a dog
a bird	Coca Cola	tea	milk
orange juice	a clock	Los Angeles	Canada
Texas	(your town)	the mountains	a park
a 747	a toaster	a farm	an apartment building
a dinosaur	a fur coat	a teacher	a doctor
a friend	ice cream	the ocean	an elephant
a diamond ring			

Writing 99

"Bigger, Better" BINGO

Listen to the teacher. Find an object on this board that can be compared to the one the teacher reads. Write a comparative sentence in the appropriate square. When you have four in a row, call out "BINGO!"

Reproducible for classroom use. Copyright © 2001 Nina Ito and Anne Berry.

Punctuation BINGO

These games teach and test students' knowledge of punctuation rules.

The BINGO Board
There is one board for this game. Students may play individually or in pairs.

The Procedure
❹ Game 1: The teacher makes a copy of the board for each student. Each student chooses a row (horizontal, vertical or diagonal) that they can punctuate correctly. When a student has completed five squares in a row, they should call out "BINGO!" To confirm the win, the student goes to the board to write the five sentences with punctuation. During this time, the other students continue to work on their sentences. If the five sentences are correct, the student is declared the winner. If any of the sentences are incorrect, the student must sit down. The game can continue so that other students can get BINGO and check their punctuation.

❹ Game 2: See Game 1, except that students can consult a style manual or textbook.

Answer Key
Row 1 They visited Phoenix, Arizona, and Denver, Colorado.
          "Do you know the answer?" she asked.
          The directions were as follows: Go three blocks south.
          Mr. Gagne asked us if we were ready.
          I'm afraid I lost your dictionary; I'll buy you another.
Row 2 She enjoys tennis, but she prefers golf.
          Did you say "I can't" or "I can?"
          I enjoy flying; however, the flight to Tokyo is too long.
          She yelled, "Quiet!"
          These students are, of course, always on time.
Row 3 I'll receive my B.A. on Dec. 15th.
          Sonia, in her last essay, improved her use of punctuation.
          "While I'm away," Teresa said, "please water my plants."
          Choose one of these side dishes: french fries or cole slaw.
          While eating, the group decided on their plan of action.
Row 4 Who, in your opinion, is the greatest athlete of all time?
          Yes, there is a "g" in the word foreign.
          You need to show up for work on time, or you will be fired.
          Tomorrow, April 8th, is our wedding anniversary.
          Never in a million years will I learn all of those rules.
Row 5 Our friends Debbie and Brian live in Detroit, Michigan.
          "Happy Birthday" is one of the most famous songs in the world.
          We're sorry, Sir, for cheating on the exam.
          "Flight No. 079 to Cleveland, Ohio, will be delayed," the voice on the loudspeaker announced.
          Dr. Terryhill lives in New Jersey now, doesn't she?

          Writing 101

Punctuation BINGO

Choose one row (horizontal, vertical, or diagonal). Add the correct punctuation to the sentences. When you are finished, call out "BINGO!"

They visited Phoenix Arizona and Denver Colorado.	Do you know the answer she asked	The directions were as follows Go three blocks south	Mr Gagne asked us if we were ready	Im afraid I lost your dictionary Ill buy you another
She enjoys tennis but she prefers golf	Did you say I cant or I can	I enjoy flying however the flight to Tokyo is too long	She yelled Quiet	These students are of course always on time
Ill receive my BA on Dec 15th	Sonia in her last essay improved her use of punctuation	While Im away Teresa said Please water my plants	Choose one of these side dishes french fries or cole slaw	While eating the group decided on their plan of action
Who in your opinion is the greatest athlete of all time	Yes there is a g in the word foreign	You need to show up for work on time or you will be fired	Tomorrow April 8th is our wedding anniversary	Never in a million years will I learn all of those rules
Our friends Debbie and Brian live in Detroit Michigan	Happy Birthday is one of the most famous songs in the world	Were sorry Sir for cheating on the exam	Flight No 079 to Cleveland Ohio will be delayed the voice on the loudspeaker announced	Dr Terryhill lives in New Jersey now doesn't she

Writing Tasks BINGO

These games can be used as a culminating activity in a writing class, or over the course of a term as extra writing practice.

The BINGO Board
There is one board for this game.

The Procedure
❹ Game 1: The teacher makes a copy of the board for each pair of students. The students read the instructions at the top of the page and begin by choosing a row (horizontal, vertical or diagonal) that has tasks that they can do quickly and well. While the students are working, the teacher circulates to clarify the tasks (e.g. "Write a limerick…"). When students have completed five tasks in a row, they should call out "BINGO!" The temptation to call out "BINGO!" quickly may cause some students to do sloppy work. The teacher can remind students to take their time.

The following scale is an example of one that can be used to determine the winners of the game.

Points for speediness:
20 points	first pair finished
15 points	second pair finished
10 points	all other pairs that finish
0 points	pairs that do not finish

Points for quality:
10 points	for each task that would receive an "A" if graded
8 points	for each task that would receive a "B" if graded
5 points	for each task that would receive a "C" if graded
0 points	for each task that is incomplete, incorrect, etc.

❹ Game 2: The teacher makes a copy of the board for each student. As an example, the teacher chooses one task for the class to complete together. Thereafter, the students work on other tasks as homework, during their free time, or when they finish an in-class activity early. Each time a student completes five tasks in a row (horizontal, vertical or diagonal), they hand them in to the teacher, who may assign points for quality (for example, see above). If the tasks are done well, the student may also receive some form of recognition (extra credit, a prize, etc.). If a student completes all 25 tasks, there can be special recognition.

Writing Tasks BINGO

Choose a row (horizontal, vertical or diagonal). Do all five tasks on separate paper. When you are finished, you have "BINGO!"

Your tasks will be judged on QUALITY, so take your time!

Write a THANK-YOU SPEECH for being elected "Class President."	Write the basic PLOT of a horror movie about a giant spider.	Write three TOPIC SENTENCES about "Benefits of Physical Exercise."	Write a short EDITORIAL about a current "hot topic."	Write an EXTENDED DEFINITION of "love."
Write a THESIS STATEMENT for an essay on doctor-assisted suicide.	Write five possible TITLES for an essay on the effects of television on children.	Write a CLASSIFIED AD to sell your textbook for this class.	Do some PRE-WRITING (use a graphic organizer) about the topic "Addicted to the Internet."	Write a LIMERICK about your teacher.
Write a NEWSPAPER ARTICLE about a ficti-tious bank robbery.	Write a SUMMARY of a recent sports event that you saw.	Write an OUTLINE for an essay on "How to Be a Good Student."	Draw and caption a CARTOON (one panel) about this class.	Write ten LINES OF DIALOGUE of a romance novel.
Write a RECIPE for a simple food from your native culture.	Write a DESCRIPTIVE PARAGRAPH about the contents of your backpack.	Write a short (6-8 lines) RAP SONG about your teacher.	Write a LESSON PLAN on how to teach low-level students to write a paragraph.	Write a LETTER to your parents about the progress you are making in learning English.
Think of a JOKE in your native language. Write it in English. (Your teacher must laugh!)	Write a HAIKU about this class today.	BRAINSTORM five reasons for raising the legal driving age to 18 (for a persuasive essay).	Write a SCRIPT for a TV commercial to sell laundry detergent.	SURVEY your classmates about their favorite color. Construct a PIE GRAPH with the results.

Ice Breaker BINGO
(First Day Activity)

These games provide practice with question formation and help students get to know each other during the first week of class.

The BINGO Board
There is one board for this game.

The Procedure
❷ ❸ ❹ The teacher makes a copy of the board for each student. In class, the students move around the room asking classmates questions in order to find someone who matches each description. For example, one square says, "Find someone who…owns a bicycle." A student would ask a classmate, "Do you own a bicycle?" If the classmate says "No", the student asks another classmate. If the classmate says "Yes", the student writes the classmate's name in that square. When a student has written a name in five squares in a row (horizontally, vertically, or diagonally), they should call out "BINGO!" To confirm the win, the student tells the class which classmates match the five descriptions.

❷ ❸ ❹ Game 2: See Game 1, except that more squares are required to get BINGO. Instead of calling out "BINGO!" when a student has written a name in the five squares of one row, they must get a name in squares that make a letter of the alphabet (for example, Z, N, T, X, or S) and then call out "BINGO!"

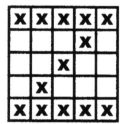 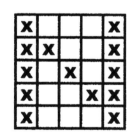 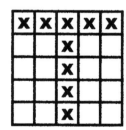 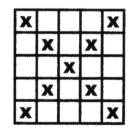 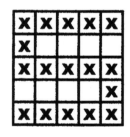

Tips for "Find Someone Who…" Activities
Before starting this activity, make sure students understand the instructions.

- Keep students circulating around the classroom to ask the questions. If possible, allow each student's name to be used only once on classmates' bingo boards.

- Stress that the students must ask the question out loud instead of merely showing the bingo board to a classmate and getting them to sign wherever appropriate.

- Don't allow the students to *congregate in groups* of 4 or more. In that situation, one student will ask a question, but three will say "Sign my sheet!" Likewise, a student shouldn't yell out any question to the whole class to find someone who says "yes."

Cultural Topics (Holidays)

Ice Breaker BINGO

Ask your classmates questions until you find someone who matches the descriptions on this board. Each time someone answers "Yes!" to your question, write his or her name in the square. You may only use one answer from each person. When you have five in a row, call out "BINGO!"

Find someone who...

... has two brothers and two sisters.	... has a friend in another ESL class here.	... has been to New York City.	... smokes.	... whose favorite color is "green."
... can dance.	... owns a used car.	... came to the U.S. more than two months ago.	... has a relative (uncle, aunt, etc.) living in the U.S.	... saw a movie in a theater last week.
... speaks a 3rd language.	... likes spicy hot food.	... wears contact lenses.	... is homesick now.	... whose family owns a cat.
...plays a musical instrument.	... likes to do homework.	... has a lucky number. What is it?	... owns a bicycle.	... likes to go shopping for clothes.
... lives with a host family.	... has a nickname. What is it?	... is tired right now.	...wants to attend a university in this country.	...reads a newspaper every day (in English).

Reproducible for classroom use. Copyright © 2001 Nina Ito and Anne Berry.

Campus Scavenger Hunt BINGO

This game helps students get to know their campus and builds team morale.

<u>The BINGO Board</u>
There is one board for this game.

<u>The Procedure</u>
❸ ❹ The teacher makes one copy of the board, and then personalizes the game by filling in specific information in the squares that have a blank line. Then the teacher makes a copy for each team of students. The teacher determines the <u>time limit</u> and the <u>number of rows</u> needed to get BINGO.

In teams, the students read the instructions at the top of the page. The students should strategize and plan their route before going out to do the scavenger hunt. The teacher should remain in the classroom in case a team comes back to ask a clarification question. When the teams have done the required number of tasks, they should return to the classroom. To confirm the win, the teacher checks the information that the students have gathered. Once all students have returned to the classroom, the group can discuss the easiest and most difficult tasks on the board.

Campus Scavenger Hunt BINGO

Work in pairs or in teams of three. You *must* stay together during the Scavenger Hunt. Your time limit is _____ minutes.

Look at the tasks below. You must do _____ rows of tasks within the time limit. It will be easier if you decide which tasks you will try *before* you go outside. Use the back of this sheet to write your answers.

If you finish before the time limit, return to the classroom. If all of your answers are correct, you get BINGO! If you have not finished by the time limit, return to the classroom anyway. The team that has the most correct answers will be the winner.

Check out a book from the campus library on this topic: *_____	Survey 10 students about their favorite place to eat on or near campus.	Find out when the next theatrical performance on campus is.	Get a course schedule for this semester. Find a class that you would like to take.	Buy a gift for your teacher from the bookstore that costs exactly 35 cents (before tax).
Go to the cafeteria in a residence hall. What is the main dinner entrée tonight?	Find out how you can join an intramural team (any sport).	Stop to have a drink. Bring the receipt to class.	Go to the parking services office. Bring back a map of parking lots that are open to students.	Get the autograph of an "important" person on campus. Why is the person important?
Find out where students can recycle aluminum cans on campus.	Send an e-mail message to your teacher. Address: *_____	Go to the campus counseling office. Get some information on *Stress Management.*.	Get a copy of the campus newspaper. Circle a classified ad for a roommate.	Find out which bus route(s) pass by campus.
Go to the campus health center. Get a pamphlet on this topic: *_____	Find an art exhibit on campus. Bring back a flyer.	Find out if the campus women's center provides guest speakers for classes.	Find a student whose birthday is in May. Have him/her sign this sheet.	Find out the hours of the campus swimming pool. How much is a daily pass?
Find out how many students from *your country* are studying in this program.	Go to the campus interfaith center. Which religions does it serve?	Get the current schedule of games for this campus team: *_____	Find out which computer lab a student can use to scan a photo for a personal web page.	Go to a language lab on campus. For which languages do they have exercises?

Valentine's Day BINGO

(Rhythm and Rhyming)

This game practices sentence stress, rhythm, and rhyming.

The BINGO Board
There is one board for this game. Students who strategize will get BINGO first. Suggestion: Photocopy the boards on *pink* paper.

The Procedure
❷ ❸ ❹ The teacher makes a copy of the board for each student or pair of students. Students choose one row (horizontal, vertical or diagonal) and write the last two lines of the poem. While the students are working, the teacher circulates to offer help. Any lines that rhyme and fit the meter (as in the examples), and that make sense, can be used to mark that square. When a student has completed the poems in three squares in a row, they should call out "BINGO!" To confirm the win, the student reads the three poems out loud while the teacher verifies that they follow the model and make sense. The game can continue so that other students can get BINGO and read their poems.

Examples:

Roses are red
*Violets are **blue***
You love me
*And I love **you****

Roses are red
*Violets are **blue***
If you don't love me
*I'll cry boo hoo **hoo***

Roses are red
*Violets are **blue***
Your love is as sweet
*As the morning **dew***

Roses are red
*Violets are **blue***
I'll love you forever
*I swear that it's **true***

Roses are red
*Violets are **blue***
Will you still love me
*When the day is **new**?*

Roses are red
*Violets are **blue***
Our family life
*Is as fun as a **zoo***

* Underlined syllables carry stress. Each line has two beats. The last words in lines two and four (bold typeface) rhyme.

Cultural Topics (Holidays) 109

Valentine's Day BINGO

Roses are red
Violets are blue
Sugar is sweet
And so are you

Choose a row (horizontal, vertical or diagonal). Write the last two lines of the poem in each square. When you are finished, call out "BINGO!"

Roses are red *Lilies are white*	*Roses are red* *Daisies are cheap*	*Roses are red* *Their leaves are green*
Roses are red *Bluebells are cute*	*Roses are red* *Carnations are pink*	*Roses are red* *Sunflowers are tall*
Roses are red *Poppies are, too*	*Roses are red* *Orchids smell great*	*Roses are red* *Daffodils are yellow*

Reproducible for classroom use. Copyright © 2001 Nina Ito and Anne Berry.

Presidents' Day BINGO

This game can be used to test students' knowledge of Abraham Lincoln and George Washington, or to start a discussion about Presidents' Day

The BINGO Boards
There are eight boards for this game. The students may play individually or in pairs. If there are more than 16 students in the class, extra boards may be photocopied. In this case, several students should get BINGO at the same time.

The Cards
Before class, the teacher should photocopy and cut apart the cards below and on the next page. The teacher can glue each rectangle to an index card to make a permanent set.

The Procedure
❸ ❹ The teacher can choose to pre-teach the information in the game or incorporate the game into a unit on presidents. Then, on Presidents' Day, the game can be played. The teacher mixes up the cards and places them face down on the table. The teacher draws the top card from the stack and reads the question. The students look at their boards, and if they have the answer, they mark the appropriate square. When a student has marked five squares in a row (horizontally, vertically, or diagonally), they should call out "BINGO!" To confirm the win, the student tells the class which five they have in a row while the teacher verifies that these are correct. Note: The center square is a "free space."

Presidents' Day BINGO	Instructions: Read the questions. Students mark the answers on their boards.	When was Lincoln born? *February 12, 1809*
When was Washington born? *February 22, 1732*	In which state was Lincoln born? *Kentucky*	In which state was Washington born? *Virginia*
In which year did Lincoln become President? *1861*	In which year did Washington become President? *1789*	On which coin is Lincoln's face? *The penny*
On which coin is Washington's face? *The quarter*	On which bill is Lincoln's face? *$5 bill*	On which bill is Washington's face? *$1 bill*
What was Lincoln's wife's name? *Mary*	What was Washington's wife's name? *Martha*	Which war is Lincoln associated with? *Civil War*

Cultural Topics (Holidays) 111

Which war is Washington associated with? *Revolutionary War*	Who was Lincoln's Vice President? *Hannibal Hamlin*	Who was Washington's Vice President? *John Adams*
Which political party did Lincoln belong to? *Republican*	Which political party did Washington belong to? *No official party*	What was Lincoln's nickname? *"Honest Abe"*
What was Washington's nickname? *"The Father of our Country"*	Which famous phrase did Lincoln say? *"Fourscore and seven years ago"*	Which famous sentence did Washington say? *"I cannot tell a lie"*
Which President (which #) was Lincoln? *#16*	Which President (which #) was Washington? *#1*	How many years was Lincoln President? *4*
How many years was Washington President? *8*	Where did Lincoln live as President? *The White House*	Where did Washington live as President? *The Presidential Palace*
What is a famous facial characteristic of Lincoln? *He had a beard.*	What is a famous facial characteristic of Washington? *He had wooden teeth.*	How did Lincoln die? *He was assassinated.*
How did Washington die? *He became ill and died.*	What job did Lincoln have when he was young? *Postmaster*	What job did Washington have when he was young? *Military Officer*
Where is Lincoln's house located? *Springfield, Illinois*	What is the name of Washington's house? *Mount Vernon*	What is the traditional food on Washington's Birthday? *Cherry Pie*
Which famous speech did Lincoln write? *Gettysburg Address*	Which day of the week is Presidents' Day? *Monday*	Why are schoolchildren happy on Presidents' Day? *Classes are cancelled.*

Reproducible for classroom use. Copyright © 2001 Nina Ito and Anne Berry.

Presidents' Day BINGO

Listen to the teacher. If you see the answer, mark the square. When you have five in a row, call out "BINGO!"

Monday	Revolutionary War	He had a beard.	Gettysburg Address	Hannibal Hamlin
February 22, 1732	Republican	He became ill and died.	Kentucky	No official party
1861	"The Father of our Country"		1789	Mount Vernon
the quarter	#16	"Fourscore and seven years ago"	Martha	"I cannot tell a lie."
Mary	8	Cherry pie	$5 bill	#1

------------------------------------✂------------------------------------

Presidents' Day BINGO

Listen to the teacher. If you see the answer, mark the square. When you have five in a row, call out "BINGO!"

John Adams	February 12, 1809	He had wooden teeth.	8	Gettysburg Address
"Honest Abe"	Virginia	He was assassinated.	#1	Military Officer
"Fourscore and seven years ago"	the penny		Mount Vernon	Classes are cancelled.
4	$1 bill	Postmaster	Revolutionary War	Martha
The White House	Civil War	The Presidential Palace	1789	Monday

Cultural Topics (Holidays)   113

Presidents' Day BINGO

Listen to the teacher. If you see the answer, mark the square. When you have five in a row, call out "BINGO!"

Classes are cancelled.	The White House	1861	Mary	He had a beard.
Postmaster	"Honest Abe"	February 12, 1809	Hannibal Hamlin	He became ill and died.
He had wooden teeth	John Adams		Republican	Military officer
#1	Civil War	Virginia	"The Father of our Country"	Cherry pie
"Fourscore and seven years ago"	$1 bill	the penny	4	Monday

------------------------------✂------------------------------

Presidents' Day BINGO

Listen to the teacher. If you see the answer, mark the square. When you have five in a row, call out "BINGO!"

He was assassinated.	$5 bill	#16	John Adams	Classes are cancelled.
February 22, 1732	Martha	He became ill and died.	"Honest Abe"	Cherry pie
Kentucky	No official party		The White House	Military officer
1789	Mount Vernon	The Presidential Palace	He had a beard.	$1 bill
the quarter	"I cannot tell a lie."	Springfield, Illinois	#1	He had wooden teeth.

Reproducible for classroom use. Copyright © 2001 Nina Ito and Anne Berry.

Presidents' Day BINGO

Listen to the teacher. If you see the answer, mark the square. When you have five in a row, call out "BINGO!"

He had wooden teeth.	Mount Vernon	1861	Kentucky	Postmaster
The Presidential Palace	"The Father of our Country"	the penny	February 12, 1809	He was assassinated.
8	No official party		Monday	Gettysburg Address
#1	Hannibal Hamlin	$5 bill	Springfield, Illinois	"Fourscore and seven years ago"
"I cannot tell a lie."	Civil War	Mary	Cherry pie	4

- ✂ -

Presidents' Day BINGO

Listen to the teacher. If you see the answer, mark the square. When you have five in a row, call out "BINGO!"

Gettysburg Address	February 22, 1732	Virginia	1789	the quarter
Civil War	Classes are cancelled.	4	Republican	$1 bill
Monday	Military Officer		"Honest Abe"	Martha
$5 bill	He was assassinated.	The White House	"Fourscore and seven years ago"	Revolutionary War
February 12, 1809	"I cannot tell a lie."	He had a beard.	#16	John Adams

Cultural Topics (Holidays) 115

Presidents' Day BINGO

Listen to the teacher. If you see the answer, mark the square. When you have five in a row, call out "BINGO!"

Civil War	Martha	$5 bill	Virginia	Hannibal Hamlin
He had a beard.	The White House	4	#16	"Fourscore and seven years ago"
He became ill and died.	February 12, 1809		He had wooden teeth.	"The Father of our Country"
Military Officer	Gettysburg Address	Classes are cancelled.	The Presidential Palace	No official party
Cherry pie	Monday	Kentucky	Republican	John Adams

- ✂ -

Presidents' Day BINGO

Listen to the teacher. If you see the answer, mark the square. When you have five in a row, call out "BINGO!"

Mount Vernon	"Honest Abe"	Hannibal Hamlin	Revolutionary War	Mary
the quarter	1861	He became ill and died.	The White House	Cherry pie
He had wooden teeth.	February 22, 1732		Virginia	8
The Presidential Palace	He was assassinated.	Postmaster	#1	Republican
Martha	the penny	Classes are cancelled.	"I cannot tell a lie."	"The Father of our Country"

"Green" BINGO for St. Patrick's Day

This game teaches students some colorful expressions and can be used for fun on St. Patrick's Day.

The BINGO Boards
There are eight boards for this game. The students may play individually or in pairs. If there are more than 16 students in the class, extra boards may be photocopied. In this case, several students should get BINGO at the same time. Suggestion: Photocopy the boards on *green* paper!

The Cards
Before class, the teacher should photocopy and cut apart the cards on the next page. The teacher can glue each rectangle to an index card to make a permanent set.

The Procedure
❸ Game 1: Each day for about a month prior to St. Patrick's Day, the teacher should write one of the "green" answers on the board and explain the meaning. Then, on St. Patrick's Day, the game can be played. The teacher mixes up the cards and places them face down on the table. The teacher draws the top card from the stack and reads the clue. The students look at their boards, and if they have the answer, they mark the appropriate square. When a student has marked four squares in a row (horizontally, vertically, or diagonally), they should call out "BINGO!" To confirm the win, the student tells the class which four they have in a row while the teacher verifies that these are correct.

❹ Game 2: See Game 1, except that the teacher does not pre-teach the expressions. On St. Patrick's Day, advanced students can use their basic knowledge to guess answers as they play.

Cultural Topics (Holidays) 117

"GREEN" Bingo for St. Patrick's Day	This is the cost of one round of golf at a particular course. *Greens fees*	This is the largest island in the world. *Greenland*
This is a permit for non-citizens to live and work in the U.S.A.. *Green card*	This is a waiting room for the actors in some theaters. *Greenroom*	This is a small building (usually made of glass) where plants and flowers grow. *Greenhouse*
This is a slang term for an inexperienced person. *Greenhorn*	This is a slang term for money . *Greenbacks*	This means that a person is good at taking care of plants. *Green thumb*
This is an international organization dedicated to the environment. *Greenpeace*	This is an area around a city preserved for parkland. *Greenbelt*	This is what the moon is made of (in jokes). *Green cheese*
This is an adjective for someone who is very jealous. *Green-eyed*	This is a person who sells fruits and vegetables. *Greengrocer*	Some of these are grapes, avocados, and limes. *Green fruits*
Some of these are lettuce, celery, and cucumbers. *Green vegetables*	These people are from the planet Mars (in jokes). *Little green men*	This is what racing car drivers do after a yellow flag. *Go on the green*
This is what Chicago does to its river on March 17th. *Turns it green*	This is what New York City paints down the middle of 5th Avenue on March 17th. *A green stripe*	This is a slang term for a person who is nauseous. *Green around the gills*
This means to get permission to do something. *Get the green light*	This means that the person has a lot of money. *With my pockets full of green*	This means that people want what others have. *The grass is always greener on the other side*

☘ *"Green" BINGO for St. Patrick's Day* ☘

Listen to the teacher. If you see the answer on this board, mark the square. When you have four in a row, call out "BINGO!"

a green stripe	little green men	green fruits	go on the green
greengrocer	green-eyed	greenbelt	Greenpeace
green around the gills	green thumb	greenhorn	greenbacks
get the green light	greenhouse	green card	Greenland

- ✂ -

☘ *"Green" BINGO for St. Patrick's Day* ☘

Listen to the teacher. If you see the answer on this board, mark the square. When you have four in a row, call out "BINGO!"

little green men	greens fees	Greenland	green card
green cheese	greenbelt	green around the gills	Greenpeace
with my pockets full of green	greenroom	greenbacks	green thumb
go on the green	The grass is always greener on the other side.	green vegetables	turns it green

Cultural Topics (Holidays) 119

🍀 *"Green" BINGO for St. Patrick's Day* 🍀

Listen to the teacher. If you see the answer on this board, mark the square. When you have four in a row, call out "BINGO!"

Greenland	greenroom	green card	greenhouse
greenhorn	get the green light	green thumb	Greenpeace
green around the gills	green cheese	green-eyed	greengrocer
green vegetables	little green men	a green stripe	go on the green

---------------------------------✂------------------------------------

🍀 *"Green" BINGO for St. Patrick's Day* 🍀

Listen to the teacher. If you see the answer on this board, mark the square. When you have four in a row, call out "BINGO!"

green fruits	go on the green	The grass is always greener on the other side.	a green stripe
turns it green	greens fees	green-eyed	greenbelt
green cheese	green around the gills	green thumb	greenbacks
get the green light	greenhouse	with my pockets full of green	green card

☘ *"Green" BINGO for St. Patrick's Day* ☘

Listen to the teacher. If you see the answer on this board, mark the square. When you have four in a row, call out "BINGO!"

greenbacks	greenhorn	get the green light	greenhouse
green card	greenroom	Greenland	with my pockets full of green
greengrocer	turns it green	green vegetables	greens fees
The grass is always greener on the other side.	go on the green	green fruits	little green men

- ✂ -

☘ *"Green" BINGO for St. Patrick's Day* ☘

Listen to the teacher. If you see the answer on this board, mark the square. When you have four in a row, call out "BINGO!"

little green men	green vegetables	greengrocer	green cheese
a green stripe	turns it green	green-eyed	greenbelt
with my pockets full of green	get the green light	greenbacks	green around the gills
greenhouse	greenhorn	green thumb	Greenpeace

Cultural Topics (Holidays) 121

☘ *"Green" BINGO for St. Patrick's Day* ☘

Listen to the teacher. If you see the answer on this board, mark the square. When you have four in a row, call out "BINGO!"

Greenland	green card	greenroom	with my pockets full of green
greenhouse	get the green light	greenhorn	greenbacks
green thumb	green around the gills	Greenpeace	greenbelt
green cheese	green-eyed	greengrocer	turns it green

------------------------------✂------------------------------

☘ *"Green" BINGO for St. Patrick's Day* ☘

Listen to the teacher. If you see the answer on this board, mark the square. When you have four in a row, call out "BINGO!"

The grass is always greener on the other side.	go on the green	green fruits	little green men
a green stripe	greens fees	greengrocer	green-eyed
green cheese	greenbelt	Greenpeace	green around the gills
green vegetables	green thumb	greenbacks	greenhorn

Earth Day BINGO

(April 22ⁿᵈ)

These games teach vocabulary, provide practice with question formation, and promote conversation.

The BINGO Board
There is one board for this game.

The Procedure
❷ ❸ Game 1: The teacher can choose to pre-teach the vocabulary in the game or incorporate the game into a unit on the Environment. The teacher makes a copy of the board for each student. In class, the students move around the room asking classmates questions in order to find someone who does each activity. For example, one square says, "Find someone who... recycles." A student would ask a classmate, "Do you recycle?" If the classmate says "No", the student asks another classmate. If the classmate says "Yes", the student writes the classmate's name in that square. When a student has written a name in four squares in a row (horizontally, vertically or diagonally), they should call out "BINGO!" To confirm the win, the student tells the class which classmates do the four activities.

Tips for "Find Someone Who..." Activities
Before starting this activity, make sure the students understand the instructions.

• Keep the students circulating around the classroom to ask the questions. If possible, allow each student's name to be used only once on classmates' bingo boards.

• Stress that the students must ask the question out loud instead of merely showing the bingo board to a classmate and getting them to sign wherever appropriate.

• Don't allow the students to *congregate in groups* of 4 or more. In that situation, one student will ask a question, but three will say "Sign my sheet!" Likewise, a student shouldn't yell out any question to the whole class to find someone who says "yes."

❷ ❸ Game 2: See Game 1, except that more squares are required to get BINGO. Instead of calling out "BINGO!" when a student has written a name in the four squares of one row, they must get a name in squares that make a letter of the alphabet (for example, Z, N, T, X, or L) and then call out "BINGO!"

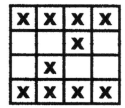 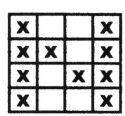 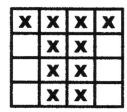 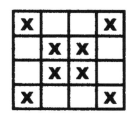 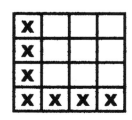

❸ ❹ Game 3: See Games 1 and 2, except that the teacher sends the students out onto the campus or into the community. Students survey native speakers until they get BINGO (either four in a row, or one of the letters in Game 2, or all sixteen squares). Once all students have returned to the classroom, the class can discuss the success of the interactions, the results of the survey and what conclusions they can draw.

Tips for Student Surveys
Before sending students out to interview native speakers, make sure that they are prepared.

• Teach students how to politely interrupt people and how to introduce themselves and their task. For example, they can say, "Excuse me. I'm an international student doing a survey for my English class. May I ask you a question?" Role-play this situation in class several times in class. Take the role of the native speaker. Be cooperative one time, but uncooperative the next (e.g. you can pretend that you're in a hurry). Tell students to say "Thank you" or "Thanks anyway." Be sure that the students ask you the question orally instead of merely showing you their bingo board.

• As a class, practice the pronunciation of all the questions or clues.

• For low-level classes, consider sending the students out of the classroom in pairs.

• Make sure that the students do not all go to the same area to survey native speakers. Plan in advance where you will send each student or pair of students.

Earth Day BINGO

Ask your classmates questions until you find someone who does the activities on this board. Each time someone answers "Yes!" to your question, write his or her name in the square. You may only use one answer from each person. When you have four in a row, call out "BINGO!"

Find someone who…

…recycles paper	…cleans up after a picnic	…keeps the house at 68°F in the winter	…is a vegetarian
…donates clothes to the poor	…rides a bicycle instead of driving a car	…uses both sides of the paper	…recycles bottles
…takes a cloth bag to the supermarket	…recycles cans	…turns off the water while brushing teeth	…uses public transportation
…turns off the lights when leaving a room	…showers in less than 5 minutes	…recycles plastic	…never litters

Labor Day BINGO
(Relative Clauses)

These games test students' knowledge of the names of professions and provides practice with relative clauses.

The BINGO Board
There is one board for this game. Eight of the squares are already filled in with professions. The students fill in the other eight squares with their choice from the list below the board or from another list that the teacher provides. In this way, every student has a different board.

The Cards
Before class, the teacher should photocopy and cut apart the cards below and on the next page. There are extra cards in case the teacher wants to add more professions to the game. The teacher can glue each rectangle to an index card to make a permanent set.

The Procedure
❶ Game 1: The teacher can choose to incorporate the game into a unit on professions or a unit on relative clauses. In either case, the teacher can pre-teach or review the vocabulary using the relative clause structure, e.g., "What does a nurse do? A nurse is a person who works with a doctor," or "…who takes care of sick people," etc. The teacher makes a copy of the board for each student. The students read the instructions and begin by filling in the blank squares on the grid. The teacher mixes up the cards and places them face down on the table. The teacher draws the top card from the stack and reads the <u>name</u> of the profession. The students look at their boards, and if they have that profession, they mark the appropriate square. When a student has marked four squares in a row (horizontally, vertically or diagonally), they should call out "BINGO!" To confirm the win, the student tells the class which four they have in a row, while the teacher verifies that these are correct.

❷ Game 2: See Game 1, except that the teacher reads the <u>description</u> of the profession. The students look at their boards, and if they have that profession, they mark the appropriate square. When a student has marked four squares in a row (horizontally, vertically or diagonally), they should call out "BINGO!" To confirm the win, the student tells the class which four they have in a row, while the teacher verifies that these are correct.

Labor Day BINGO	
a nurse	… is a person who takes care of patients in a hospital.
a pilot	… is a person who flies airplanes.
a writer	… is a person who writes articles or books.

a firefighter	…is a person who fights fires.
a garbage collector	…is a person who takes other people's garbage to the landfill.
a journalist	…is a person who investigates and writes newspaper articles.
a mail carrier	…is a person who delivers letters and packages.

a professor	...is a person who teaches at a university.	*a mechanic*	...is a person who fixes cars and other vehicles.
a truck driver	...is a person who transports goods in a truck.	*a miner*	...is a person who extracts metals and minerals from underground.
a farmer	...is a person who works the land growing crops or raising animals.	*a musician*	...is a person who plays a musical instrument or sings.
a butcher	...is a person who prepares meat for sale.	*an office worker*	...is a person who works (filing, faxing, typing) in an office.
a baker	...is a person who makes bread and other pastries.	*a photographer*	...is a person who takes pictures with a camera.
an architect	...is a person who designs houses and buildings.	*a police officer*	...is a person who fights crime and keeps the city safe.
an artist	...is a person who paints or sculpts or writes or makes music.	*a politician*	...is a person who campaigns for a job in the government.
an athlete	...is a person who practices one or more sports.	*a shop clerk*	...is a person who helps customers make purchases in a store.
a business-man/woman	...is a person who works in the world of business.	*a soldier*	...is a person who fights for a country, for example, in the army.
a barber	...is a person who cuts men's hair.	*a street cleaner*	...is a person who keeps the city clean.
a carpenter	...is a person who builds things made of wood.	*a waiter/ a waitress*	...is a person who serves food in a restaurant.
a chemist	...is a person who works in a laboratory with chemicals.		
a chef	...is a person who prepares food in a restaurant.		
a computer programmer	...is a person who writes computer software.		
a construction worker	...is a person who does physical work involved with building.		
a doctor	...is a person who examines patients and prescribes medicines.		
a factory worker	...is a person who works in a factory.		

Labor Day *BINGO*

Fill in each blank square with a type of profession from the list below. Then listen to the teacher. Mark the square with the profession you hear. When you have four in a row, call out "BINGO!"

Professions

Architect	Construction worker	Musician
Artist	Doctor	Office worker
Athlete	Factory worker	Photographer
Barber	Fireman	Police officer
Businessman / -woman	Garbage collector	Politician
Carpenter	Journalist	Shop clerk
Chemist	Mail carrier	Soldier
Chef	Mechanic	Street cleaner
Computer programmer	Miner	Waiter

Halloween Riddle BINGO

This game enhances students' cultural knowledge of a popular U.S. holiday and exposes them to riddles and plays on words.

The BINGO Boards
There are eight boards for this game. The students may play individually or in pairs. If there are more than 16 students in the class, extra boards may be photocopied. In this case, several students should get BINGO at the same time. Suggestion: Photocopy the boards on orange paper!

The Cards
Before class, the teacher should photocopy and cut apart the cards below and on the next page. The teacher can glue each rectangle to an index card to make a permanent set.

The Procedure
❹ Before class, the teacher must decide whether to explain the riddles before, during or after the game. The teacher mixes up the cards and places them face down on the table. The teacher draws the top card from the stack and reads the riddle. The students look at their boards, and if they have the answer, they mark the appropriate square. When a student has marked five squares in a row (horizontally, vertically or diagonally), they should call out "BINGO!" To confirm the win, the student tells the class which five they have in a row, while the teacher verifies that these are correct. Note: The center square is a "free space."

HALLOWEEN RIDDLE BINGO	What do you call a witch who lives at the beach? *A sand-witch*	What kind of witch turns out the light? *A lights-witch*
What did the witch ask for at the hotel? *Broom service*	What does a witch do when she's sleepy? *She takes a cat nap.*	Why does a witch know everybody's secrets? *Because she's nosey.*
Where do baby ghosts spend their days? *Day scare centers*	Who did the ghost invite to his party? *Anyone he could dig up*	What kind of make-up do ghosts wear? *Mas-scare-a*
Where do ghosts like to shop? *Boo-tiques*	What's a ghost's favorite dessert? *I-scream*	What's a ghost's favorite ride at the amusement park? *The roller ghoster*
What was the name of the ghost motel? *Rest-Inn-Peace*	What is a ghost's favorite fruit? *Boo-berries*	What does the Mother Ghost read to her baby? *Scary Tales*
Why did the police officer arrest the ghost? *Because he didn't have a haunting license.*	Where do vampires keep their money? *In a blood bank*	Where does Count Dracula go water skiing? *In Lake Eerie*

Cultural Topics (Holidays) 129

How can you tell that a vampire likes baseball? *He turns into a bat every night.*	Which song does Count Dracula hate? *"Sunshine on my Shoulders"*	What kind of dog does Count Dracula have? *A blood-hound*
How does a girl vampire flirt? *She bats her eyes.*	What's it like to be kissed by a vampire? *It's a pain in the neck.*	What's a vampire's favorite fruit? *A neck-tarine*
Why did Count Dracula visit the school cafeteria? *He dropped in for a quick bite.*	What do you call twin boy vampires? *Blood brothers*	Why does Count Dracula go bowling in the evening? *Because he only strikes at night.*
What animal flies around a school at night? *The alphabat*	What do you call a baby monster's parents? *Mummy and Deady*	What did the monster eat at the restaurant? *Two waiters and a busboy*
What's a monster's favorite bean? *A human "bean"*	What bill does a monster pay on Halloween? *The electrick bill*	How many cookies can a monster eat? *As many as he wants*
How do mummies hide? *They wear masking tape.*	Where do mummies go for a swim? *The Dead Sea*	Why doesn't a skeleton use a towel after taking a shower? *He always comes out bone dry.*
How do you make a skeleton laugh? *Hit him in the funny bone.*	Why didn't the skeleton go to the dance? *Because he didn't have any body to go with.*	Who won the skeleton beauty contest? *No body*
What musical instrument does a skeleton play? *The trom-bone*	What do skeletons say before they begin dinner? *Bone-appetit*	How do werewolves greet each other? *Howl do you do?*
What's worse than a bald werewolf? *A toothless vampire*	Where does the Wolfman live? *In Howllywood, California*	What is Beethoven doing in his grave? *De-composing*
What did the devil give his girlfriend? *A 2-carat demon*	Why did the spider get a ticket? *He was weaving through traffic.*	Why do cemeteries have fences around them? *People are dying to get in.*
Why did the doctor tell the zombie to get some rest? *He was dead on his feet.*	What did the Jack-o-Lantern say on Halloween night? *Nothing. Pumpkins can't talk.*	What do you call two witches who share an apartment? *Broom-mates*

HALLOWEEN RIDDLE BINGO

Listen to the teacher. If you see the answer to the riddle on this board, mark the square. When you have five in a row, call out "BINGO!"

Because she always comes out bone dry.	Because he didn't have a haunting license.	She takes a cat nap.	I-scream	He dropped in for a quick bite.
A neck-tarine	Mummy and Deady	She bats her eyes.	Mas-scare-a	Hit him in the funny bone.
A toothless vampire	Rest-Inn-Peace		It's a pain in the neck.	Because she's nosey.
Bone appetit	He was dead on his feet.	The Dead Sea	A sand-witch	Broom service
The electrick bill	Because he didn't have any body to go with.	The alphabat	In a blood bank	Scary Tales

--------------------------------✂--------------------------------

HALLOWEEN RIDDLE BINGO

Listen to the teacher. If you see the answer to the riddle on this board, mark the square. When you have five in a row, call out "BINGO!"

Because he only strikes at night.	The roller ghoster	As many as he wants	A lights-witch	He was weaving through traffic.
In Howllywood, California	Because people are dying to get in.	No body	The trom-bone	De-composing
Howl do you do?	"Sunshine on my Shoulders"		Two waiters and a busboy	Blood brothers
He turns into a bat every night.	They wear masking tape.	Boo-Berries	Anyone he could dig up	In Lake Eerie
A 2-carat demon	Boo-tiques	Scary Tales	A blood hound	Day scare centers

Cultural Topics (Holidays) 131

HALLOWEEN RIDDLE BINGO

Listen to the teacher. If you see the answer to the riddle on this board, mark the square. When you have five in a row, call out "BINGO!"

As many as he wants	Because he didn't have any body to go with.	Howl do you do?	Because people are dying to get in.	He was weaving through traffic.
A lights-witch	Two waiters and a busboy	In Howllywood, California	De-composing	Nothing. Pumpkins can't talk.
Rest-Inn-Peace	Because he only strikes at night.		The Dead Sea	He dropped in for a quick bite.
Mummy and Deady	It's a pain in the neck.	A blood-hound	Mas-scare-a	They wear masking tape.
She takes a cat nap.	Because he was dead on his feet.	A toothless vampire	Broom service	The alphabat

- ✂ -

HALLOWEEN RIDDLE BINGO

Listen to the teacher. If you see the answer to the riddle on this board, mark the square. When you have five in a row, call out "BINGO!"

"Sunshine on my Shoulders"	Because she always comes out bone dry.	She bats her eyes.	A 2-carat demon	A neck-tarine
He turns into a bat every night.	A sand-witch	Hit him in the funny bone.	Anyone he could dig up	I-scream
Boo-berries	Blood brothers		Broom-mates	Because she's nosey.
A human "bean"	Because he didn't have a haunting license.	In a blood bank	Day scare centers	In Lake Eerie
Howl do you do?	Boo-tiques	The electrick bill	Bone-appetit	She takes a cat nap.

HALLOWEEN RIDDLE BINGO

Listen to the teacher. If you see the answer to the riddle on this board, mark the square. When you have five in a row, call out "BINGO!"

She takes a cat nap.	The roller ghoster	Scary Tales	The Dead Sea	A 2-carat demon
No body	Two waiters and a busboy	Because people are dying to get in.	Because he didn't have a haunting license.	It's a pain in the neck.
He dropped in for a quick bite.	In Howllywood, California	(ghost image)	Boo-tiques	Hit him in the funny bone.
The trom-bone	De-composing	The electick bill	"Sunshine on my Shoulders"	Broom-mates
A toothless vampire	Nothing. Pumpkins can't talk.	He was weaving through traffic.	He turns into a bat every night.	Howl do you do?

- ✂ -

HALLOWEEN RIDDLE BINGO

Listen to the teacher. If you see the answer to the riddle on this board, mark the square. When you have five in a row, call out "BINGO!"

The alphabat	A blood-hound	Because she's nosey.	Broom-service	Boo-berries
Day scare centers	Because he didn't have any body to go with.	A lights-witch	They wear masking tape.	A neck-tarine
As many as he wants	In Lake Eerie	(pumpkin image)	Blood brothers	Because he only strikes at night.
Rest-Inn-Peace	A sand-witch	Mas-scare-a	Because he was dead on his feet.	I-scream
Bone-Appetit	In a blood bank	Because she always comes out bone dry.	Mummy and Deady	A toothless vampire

HALLOWEEN RIDDLE BINGO

Listen to the teacher. If you see the answer to the riddle on this board, mark the square. When you have five in a row, call out "BINGO!"

A human "bean"	Nothing. Pumpkins can't talk.	She takes a cat nap.	He dropped in for a quick bite.	Because she's nosey.
Rest-Inn-Peace	A toothless vampire	The electrick bill	The alphabat	Scary Tales
Hit him in the funny bone.	She bats her eyes.		Broom service	Mummy and Deady
Bone-appetit	Anyone he could dig up	A lights-switch	They wear masking tape.	A neck-tarine
A blood-hound	The roller ghoster	Mas-scare-a	Because he was dead on his feet.	I-scream

- ✄ -

HALLOWEEN RIDDLE BINGO

Listen to the teacher. If you see the answer to the riddle on this board, mark the square. When you have five in a row, call out "BINGO!"

Because he only strikes at night.	In a blood bank	Boo-tiques	He turns into a bat every night.	As many as he wants
Broom-mates	In Lake Eerie	"Sunshine on my Shoulders"	The trom-bone	Because people are dying to get in.
Howl do you do?	A sand-witch		Because he didn't have any body to go with.	He was weaving through traffic.
Day scare centers	It's a pain in the neck.	Boo-berries	In Howllywood, California	No body
A 2-carat demon	Because he didn't have a haunting license.	Scary Tales	Two waiters and a busboy	Blood brothers

Reproducible for classroom use. Copyright © 2001 Nina Ito and Anne Berry.

Thanksgiving Food BINGO

This game teaches vocabulary and enhances students' cultural knowledge of a popular U.S. holiday.

The BINGO Board
There is one board for this game.

The Procedure
❷ The teacher makes a copy of the board for each student or pair of students. The students read the instructions at the top of the page. The teacher sends the students out onto the campus or into the community to ask native speakers the question, "On Thanksgiving Day, what is your favorite thing to eat?" If someone's answer is on the board, that person should sign his or her name in that square. If an answer is not on the board, the student should write the name of the food below the board. The teacher should remind the students that they can only use one answer from each person they ask. When students have marked five squares in a row (horizontally, vertically or diagonally), they should return to the classroom and show the teacher that they got BINGO. Once all students have returned to the classroom, the group can discuss the most popular items on the board and the other foods mentioned.

Thanksgiving Food BINGO

Survey people on the street.

Question: On Thanksgiving Day, what is your favorite thing to eat?

If an answer is on this board, ask the person to sign the square. If an answer is not on the board, write it below. You may only use one answer from each person. When you have five answers in a row, you have BINGO. Return to the classroom and show your teacher.

Pumpkin Pie	Potato Salad	Jello Salad	Sweet Potatoes	Apple Pie
Cranberry Sauce	Bread	Carrots	Rolls	Yams or Candied Yams
Ham	Stuffed Mushrooms	Turkey	Corn or Creamed Corn	Gravy
Stuffing or Dressing	Corn Bread	Broccoli	Biscuits	Green Beans or Green Bean Casserole
Pecan Pie	Green Salad	Mashed Potatoes	Fruit Salad	Mincemeat Pie

December Holidays BINGO
(Christmas, Hanukkah and Kwanzaa)

This game enhances students' knowledge of three December holidays and their symbols, and can promote discussion of diversity in ethnic celebrations.

The BINGO Board
There is one board for this game. Seventeen of the squares are already filled in with holiday symbols. The students fill in the other eight squares with their choices from the list below the board. In this way, every student has a different board.

The Cards
Before class, the teacher should photocopy and cut apart the cards below and on the next page. The teacher can glue each rectangle to an index card to make a permanent set.

The Procedure
❷ The teacher can choose to pre-teach the information in this game or incorporate the game into a unit on December holidays. The teacher mixes up the cards and places them face down on the table. The teacher draws the top card from the stack and reads the clue. The students look at their boards, and if they have that picture, they mark the appropriate square. When a student has marked five squares in a row (horizontally, vertically or diagonally), they should call out "BINGO!" To confirm the win, the student tells the class which five they have in a row while the teacher verifies that these are correct.

December Holidays BINGO (Christmas, Hanukkah and Kwanzaa)	This is a peppermint stick that people eat around Christmas. *Candy Cane*	This is a figure that children build outside in December. *Snowman*
These are the traditional colors of Hanukkah. *Blue & White*	These are the traditional colors of Christmas. *Red & Green*	These are the traditional colors of Kwanzaa. *Black, Red & Green*
This is a typical food for Hanukkah. It's made from a vegetable. *Potato Pancakes*	This is a typical drink for Christmas. *Eggnog*	This is a typical food for Hanukkah. The shape is round. *Jelly Doughnuts*

These animals pull Santa Claus' sleigh on Christmas Eve. *Reindeer*	This is a greeting used during Kwanzaa. *"Harbari Gani"*	This is Santa Claus' transportation on Christmas Eve. *Sleigh*
This is the candle holder used during Hanukkah. *Menorah*	This food represents "children" during the days of Kwanzaa. *Ears of corn*	This is what the head of the family drinks from during a celebration for Kwanzaa.. *Unity Cup*
This is the popular name given to Hanukkah. *"The Festival of Lights"*	This is the date of Christmas. *December 25th*	These are the dates of Kwanzaa. *December 26th to January 1st*
This is what people send to family and friends during the Christmas season. *Christmas cards*	This is how long Hanukkah lasts. *Eight nights*	This is where Santa Claus lives. *The North Pole*
This is a decoration for a Christmas tree. *Ornament*	This is a geometric shape that is used for Christmas and Hanukkah. *Star*	If two people stand under this, they have to kiss. *Mistletoe*
This is a gift of food for Christmas, but most people don't like to eat it. *Fruitcake*	This is a toy that is given at Hanukkah and used in a game of chance. *Dreidel*	This is a Christmas decoraton that can also be a musical instrument. (You shake them.) *Jingle Bells*
These are what people give to family and friends on Christmas Day. *Presents*	These are what people study on the seven nights of Kwanzaa. *Seven principles*	This is the object kept burning by the miracle celebrated on the Feast of Hanukkah. *Lamp of Oil*

December Holidays BINGO

Fill in each blank square with a holiday item. Then listen to the teacher. Mark the square with the item you hear. When you have five in a row, call out "BINGO!"

	Candy Cane	**Black, Red & Green**		Snowman
Presents	The North Pole		December 25th	
Red & Green		*The Festival of Lights*	Seven Principles	Ornaments
	December 26th to January 1st	Eggnog		Eight Nights
Jelly Donuts		*"Harbari Gani"*	Christmas Cards	**Blue & White**

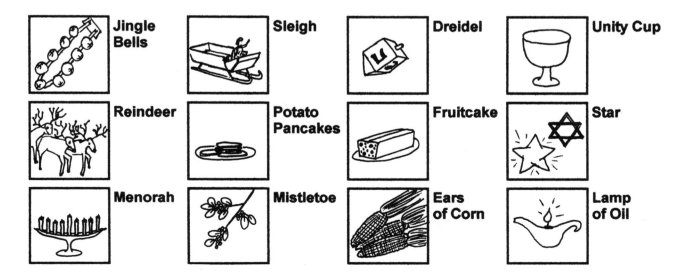

Jingle Bells   Sleigh   Dreidel   Unity Cup

Reindeer   Potato Pancakes   Fruitcake   Star

Menorah   Mistletoe   Ears of Corn   Lamp of Oil

   Cultural Topics (Holidays) 139

Chips

Photocopy this page. Mount or laminate and cut apart. Give chips to students to mark their boards.

"Make Your Own" BINGO

The BINGO Boards

The following pages contain blank grids with 9, 16, and 25 blank squares.

• If the game is to be played with one board, the teacher should make one photocopy of the blank board, fill in the information needed for the game, and then photocopy one board for each student or pair of students.

• If the game is to be played with multiple boards, the teacher should make multiple photocopies of the blank board, fill in the information needed for the game on all the boards, and then photocopy enough boards for each student or pair of students.

The Cards

The teacher should make a photocopy of the page with the blank teachers' cards, fill in the information needed for the game, and then cut apart the cards. The teacher can glue each rectangle to an index card to make a permanent set.

The Procedure

The teacher can follow the models in this book, or come up with new games.

Teacher's Cards for "Make Your Own" BINGO

Photocopy this page. Fill in the squares with your clues. Cut apart the cards and glue each rectangle to an index card to make a permanent set.

Reproducible for classroom use. Copyright © 2001 Nina Ito and Anne Berry.

_____ **BINGO**

Instructions:

- ✂ -

_____ **BINGO**

Instructions:

_____ BINGO

Instructions:

Reproducible for classroom use. Copyright © 2001 Nina Ito and Anne Berry.

_____ **BINGO**

Instructions:

Other Books of Interest from Pro Lingua

Index Card Games for ESL — A collection of six kinds of games. This is a teacher resource that tells how to play the game and provides sample games at elementary, intermediate, and advanced skill levels.

More Index Card Games — Nine more games that use index cards. Sample games are included at three skill levels. Many are copyable.

Pronunciation Card Games — Index card games that focus on pronunciation. Practicing minimal pairs, stress placement, rhythm, and intonation is fun and lively with these games.

Match It! — A collection of index card games for learners of English based on the popular game Matched Pairs, a variation of Concentration. Games practice basic vocabulary, verbs, prefixes, synonyms/antonyms, important everyday survival vocabulary, and more advanced material like compounds, collocations, idioms, and proverbs.

Solo, Duo, Trio — Puzzles and games for individual students or small groups. Builds vocabulary; photocopyable for handouts.

Operations in English — 55 natural and logical sequences for language acquisition. These are often humorous game-like classroom activities in which students working in pairs communicate naturally and accurately to accomplish set tasks, step by step.

Families — 10 card games for language learners working with basic vocabulary and question and answer structures.

Shenanigames — Grammar-focused, interactive ESL/EFL activities and games providing practice with a full range of grammar structures from the basic to the advanced.

Play 'n Talk — Comunicative games for Elementary and Middle School ESL/EFL students covering basic vocabulary, basic communicative situations, some intermediate vocabulary, verbs, adjectives, writing and spelling.

Other Books of Interest from Pro Lingua

Lexicarry — An illustrated vocabulary builder that includes sections on functions, sequences, related actions, operations, topics, proverbs, and places. Vocabulary is learned in cooperative, active, game-like activities.

Discovery Trail — An ESL/EFL board game with 900 questions practicing three levels of intermediate grammar, idioms, phrasal verbs, preposition, proverbs, U.S. and world facts in geography and history, and U.S. citizenship.

The Interactive Tutorial — An activity parade of fun, photocopyable activities for the adult ESL/EFL student in a tutorial or small group class. Easily used by tutors with or without experience or training.

Rhymes 'n Rhythms — 32 new and original rhythmic rhymes for reading or saying aloud in the classroom individually or chorally. Cassette available.

Pearls of Wisdom: African and Caribbean Folktales — For reading and listening, 12 classic tales are collected in a beautifully illustrated reader and read aloud on two cassettes by traditional storyteller Raouf Mama. An integrated language-skills workbook offers a variety of interactive activities.

Breaking the Writing Barrier — Dozens of fun activities for adolescents designed to get even the hard-to-reach students to write and enjoy it.

Write for You — Fun, creative activities for building writing skills for high school and adult students. Photocopyable.

Writing Inspirations — A Fundex of individualized activities for English language practice.

Conversation Inspirations — over 2000 conversation topics. Photocopyable.

The ESL Miscellany — A copyable teacher resource book that contains lots of lists with thousands of words that can be consulted for making index card games. There are also lists of grammar points, cultural information, communicative functions, situations, and 60 topical lists. This is Pro Lingua's most popular book, often called "the classic teacher resource" by ESL and EFl teachers.

www.ProLinguaAssociates.com • 800-366-4775